Indian Summer

A Sailing Adventure

by

Jerry & Marion Solom

We dedicate this book
to the memory of our parents:
Helmer and Inez Solom,
Melvin and Helen Hagen,
who instilled in us an appreciation
for our Scandinavian heritage.

Table of Contents

Foreword -- 5

Acknowledgment --- 8

The Beginning --- 8

I Start to Build My Boat December 1985------------------- 10

Sailing Practice Begins on *Popeye* 1986------------------- 13

Building Continues --- 14

Sailing Practice in New Orleans --------------------------- 22

A Lucky Break, *Indian Summer* Finds a Ride to the

Mississippi River, the Christening and Road Trip ------- 24

Dragging *Indian Summer* Out of

Portage Des Sioux 1994--- 31

The First Sail on *Indian Summer* --------------------------- 37

Marion Sails for the First Time on *Indian Summer*------- 39

Sailing with Jack and Charlie to the Dry Tortugas ------ 40

Sailing to Cuba and Back --------------------------------- 51

Re-Sandblasting the Hull in New Orleans --------------- 71

Gathering Crew for Norway ----------------------------- 74

2000 the Trip to Norway Begins -------------------------- 77

2001 Vacation Boot Camp, Cruising

the Coast of Norway--- 101

2002 Shetland to Portugal---------------------------------- 108

December 2002 Boat is Damaged in Portugal ----------- 121

2003 Six Weeks in Portugal -------------------------------- 122

2004 Portugal to Sada, Northern Spain -------------------- 128

2005 Sada to Kilrush, Ireland ----------------------------- 134

2006 A Non-Cruising Summer ----------------------------- 155

2007 Kilrush to Norway ------------------------------------ 158

2008 The Trip Back to America --------------------------- 170

2012 Maine to Nantucket and Martha's Vineyard ------ 186

2013 Sailing Adventures in Maine ------------------------ 217

Reflections-- 242

*Another book *Indian Summer A Sailing Adventure in Photos* is also available.

FOREWORD

In many ways this is a very unlikely story. Even now after being involved for over 28 years, I still find it hard to believe it was actually done. The main idea was done plus a host of other adventures. That is not to say there weren't any problems, but one way or another we got over them and continued on. A lot can happen in 28 years.

This sailing dream came out of thin air, and it required spending money and time I really didn't think I had. And, of course, how would I convince my wife of 19 years to believe I could do this? I didn't even try do that.

This project, I knew had to include three main points.

The first point required building a steel boat from scratch and then sailing it to Norway, the birthplace of our roots. The second point was to use this boat to visit other countries before and after my visit to Norway. I was not going to do this as some kind of stunt, but as a means to travel about. Thirdly, I didn't want any sponsors, as they would have an agenda, and I had mine. I wanted to go where I wanted and stop when I felt like stopping.

When I finally got into building and reading about boat voyaging, my heroes became Joshua Slocum, Harry Pigeon, Dwight Long, Eric & Susan Hiscocks and H.W. Tilman. They all did extensive traveling on small boats, and their adventures were so interesting to me as they took the time to stop and get to know people on their travels.

Before I got started, I owned only a 15-foot canoe and knew nothing of sailing or navigation, but I did have a love for the water and adventure.

It was dangerous when I first started trying to learn on my own, but I read extensively and practiced a lot with the first sailboat I bought even though it was not what I needed. In a couple of years, I passed the skipper's license to take up to six paying passengers sailing, and also improved the first sailboat by adding a reliable engine and stronger rig. This allowed me to sail in tougher conditions and gain valuable experience. I also took first aid classes and studied ham radio to gain an expert class license. I did all this to prepare for the trip across the ocean. It is hard to know when the boat and skipper are really ready, but in the year 2000 I had been sailing my little 26 footer and the *Indian Summer* boat for a total of 14 years, and my age of 55 added up to the time to go.

This is a collection of stories of the building and voyaging of *Indian Summer*.

First, here is a little background information. I started my education in Greenbush, Minnesota in 1951. In 1955, my folks moved to Wannaska, Minnesota where I continued to the 8th grade. In 1960, my folks moved to Roseau, Minn. where I graduated from high school in 1963. I attended Bemidji State College for two years, but dropped out in 1965, and found a job. I had been dating Marion Hagen from Roseau during my senior year in school, and we were still dating. She also attended Bemidji College. We were there together for one year. After I quit, she continued one more year and also quit. We were married in 1966.

In 1967, we moved to southern California so I could attend aircraft mechanic school, from which I graduated in 1969. I went to work for Western Airlines after graduation and worked for them about six years. In 1976, we had seen all of southern California we wanted and moved back to northern Minnesota by Wannaska, where we bought a small farm and moved in an old farm house to live in. By starting my welding business there, I was also restarting my father's business as he had sold his welding business two years before. My grandfather also had a welding business in Greenbush, about twenty miles away, for many years. I guess it was in my blood to return to it.

We are lucky to have four kids now, two born in California and two after we moved back to Minnesota. I'm happy to report that I have also been fortunate to have many of the family join us in voyaging at one time or another.

Acknowledgment

There are many adventurous people who became involved in these voyages either as sailors or land support team. First of all is my wife, Marion; son, Terry; daughters, Sara, Mary, and Erin. Other important people were Hank and Virginia Henderson, Joe McDonnell, Dale Hanson, Boyd Olmsted, Jack Davidson, Bob Carlson, Matt McDonnell, Charlie Viken, Clink and Ret Wilson, Al Gjerde, Roger Anderson, Jim Miller, Bill Landby and the LOWRA ham radio members, Keith Severson, Steven Reynolds, Stewart Mickleson, Ben & Michael Nelson, Joey McDonnell, Alex Yamrik, John Carstens, Chuck & Bruce Droogsma, Steve Johnson, John & Mallori Bouchard. Very few of these adventurers had any knowledge of sailing, but all had an abundance of courage and a desire to see what lies beyond the horizon. I was impressed with their spirit to explore.

I also need to again express my gratitude to Marion and our daughter Sara, for all the help they have given me in getting this book to print. Without them it never would have happened. I also must thank our son Terry, for twice quitting his jobs to sail on both Atlantic crossings, knowing full well it was not going to be a vacation.

The Beginning

So it all started on a routine trip in 1985, from our home by Wannaska, Minnesota to Grand Forks, North Dakota, a distance of 110 miles. On the way, we normally pass through Thief River Falls. I had no reason to believe this day would have such a huge change of direction in my life, but as we passed through TRF, we saw a large sailboat for sale parked on the side of the road. Well, I thought it was large at the time.

I had a passing interest in boats, and water has always held an interest for me. Once when we lived in California, I actually did go look at a sailboat for sale. I thought it seemed too complicated and expensive at the time. I had a couple of hobbies, motorcycling and hunting, and didn't think I needed any more distractions. But that was a few years ago, and now I told Marion I'd like to drive around the block and look at this boat. It had a look of adventure to it. Marion was quick to point out that since we were running late for an appointment and I wasn't going to buy it anyway, why spend the time looking. I continued around the block, we parked the car, and I walked up to the boat. It looked big on the trailer, and I wished I knew something about sailing. It could be a big adventure taking this boat out on the lake or even on the ocean. I don't think we talked to the owner at that time, but I was trying to think of a way I could learn something about sailing.

After we got home, I looked for someone to give me sailing lessons. I found a couple, Hank and Virgina, in a neighboring town about 40 miles away, that had taught sailing in the past, and I gave them a call. Yes, they had a sailboat, but were not teaching sailing anymore. However, they said if I bought my own boat they would be happy to rent me a slip on their dock. I believe they had the only sailboat on this side of the lake, and if I were to learn sailing, it would be by myself and on my own boat. I couldn't keep that used boat out of my mind and in a couple of weeks I couldn't hold off any longer, I bought it. When I brought it home, it was October and time for boats to be hauled out of the water. It was too late to launch my new, used boat. Well, I didn't know anything about sailing anyway, so that winter I studied all I could. The more I studied about boats, the more informed I got and realized my new used boat was what they call a day sailor. It was OK for lake sailing but not something to trust out in the ocean. By this time, I had already mentally jumped from lake sailing, to sailing to Norway, the country of our roots. Now, I thought, that would really be an adventure!

I Start to Build My Boat December 1985

The more I read, the more I realized what I really needed was a 40-foot boat. I had bought a 26-foot boat which was very basic, and it was about all I could afford. In my reading, I came across a booklet listing boat plans one could buy. They had boats from 19-feet to 62-feet. What was interesting to me was that boats from 28-feet and larger could be built of steel. For the past 10 years, I had run a metal shop where I had custom repaired and built steel projects for customers. I was certain I would be able to make any of the boats listed in the catalog.

By early December, I had decided to try to build one of the boats, and I would use the boat I bought as a trainer. I hadn't yet launched the boat I had bought only three months before. Well, it was winter and the ice was still pretty thick up here. It would take me years to build the boat and in the meantime I'd teach myself how to sail. I had studied the catalog over and had narrowed it down to two plans. One was a 38-foot and the other a 53-foot. I was hoping to have Marion's help in choosing one. When I sat with her and opened up the catalog to go over the plans, she indicated she didn't know enough about boats to know what she would like. I realized then that this was going to be my project.

I ordered the plans, for the 38-footer the next day, a Bruce Roberts design. They came by late December. I was lucky to get a discount on the plans, 50% off, that brought the cost down to $200. That seemed expensive enough, and I almost decided to forego the plans altogether and draw up my own. In retrospect, I'm sure I would have built a tight and good-looking boat, but I'm also sure it would have been a disaster. Now I realize that balance is very important to steering and performance, and that *Indian Summer* is perfectly balanced is no accident. The 200 dollars was well worth every last cent.

I started building the boat frames in February of 1986. Sailboats are rare in this part of the county, and I did feel a bit foolish building not just a sailboat, but also an ocean sailboat. As I built the frames, I would hide them out back of the shop. I didn't want to try explaining anything to my customers yet. By the spring time, all the frames, 28 of them, were done. Next, was to build a strong back to mount the frames on. This was made of wood and has uprights about three feet high that the frames are attached to. It was exciting to see the boat take shape. It may have been around this time Marion realized I was building the boat, but didn't say much, and I sure wasn't going to ask what she thought. I felt I already knew.

During the summer I installed the longitudinal and cut steel plates to hang on each side. I would alternate putting the plates on each side to keep the weight balanced on the uprights. Just the shell would weigh two ton when finished.

I didn't really have much lifting power save an old drag line. It was a bit much for the 3- by 10-foot plates so a lot of the work was done by handyman jacks and levers. By hook or crook, I would get each piece up and in place. Sometimes I got the kids and Marion to help if I needed an extra hand. They were not nearly as enthused as I was, but they would help. Maybe they thought it might happen. All this time I was still working for customers fixing and building their projects too.

In May, I also launched the 26-footer to begin my sailing lessons. From the very beginning, at the launch site there was trouble. The first launch ramp was not deep enough to get the boat to float off the trailer. That I picked opening fishing day, was a disaster in the making. There were tons of people around and many boats waiting to get put in. I finally gave up and went to another ramp further away, and there the ramp was steep enough. In fact, it was so steep that the nose of the boat got stuck on the winch as the back end of the boat lifted with the water. Finally, after much work, we got her off the trailer and tied to the side of the dock. Now the engine wouldn't start. I had invited family to go sailing, and it was a blessing the engine wouldn't start. We would have been aground before we even got out into the lake. Finally, we did get towed over to an open slip, and there we all ate our sandwiches and resolved that this was the adventure of the day. Marion's brother-in-law, who was eager to help, said when leaving not to bother calling him next time I needed help. I was very disappointed. I had done so much reading during the winter, I was sure I could sail. Now I realized how hard this was all going to be. That I had started the big boat too, made it look like I had bit off way more that I could handle. I was glad to leave the boat that day. But it seems that when I have a bad day, it doesn't take long before things turn around and look better. Too much stress does this, I think, and after a good night's rest, things did look better.

I went back to building the big boat, something I could do. A week later, I got Joe McDonnell, a neighbor friend who knew something about sailing, and Hank Henderson, the owner of the dock I was going to tie to, help me take *Liv,* the 26-footer to Hank's place about three miles away. Hank had arranged for his neighbor to come looking for us if we didn't show up by a certain time and tow us in. We did get in an hour or so of sailing, and it was great! I could feel it was right in my bones!

Sailing Practice Begins on *Popeye* 1986

I had defied superstition and renamed the boat *Popeye.* I practiced sailing that summer, and had one memorable trip, where I took the whole family out for a pleasant cruise. We had the wind from behind, and as we got farther from shore, I began to wonder how it would go returning. I turned the boat around and found we could sail back no problem, so we returned to the original course and continued sailing out into the lake. This lake is quite large, and there are about 25 miles of open water north to south, and 30 to 40 miles east to west, before islands start. So heading out into the lake was formidable for a new sailor. After a few hours we decided that sailing back would be a good idea as the wind had picked up anyway.

In turning around, I found that with the increase of wind, I could not sail as close to the course as I wanted, so I sailed off course and in due time had to make up the easting I had so freely given up. My plan was to use the engine. However, with the boat heeled over so much, the engine propeller was out of the water, needless to say, the crew, Marion and the kids were becoming tired of all this sailing and wanted to get to shore. It was a lesson in sailing for all of us. Sometimes you can't get there from here. Tacking with the engine out of the water and running the engine on the other tack that buried the engine propeller; we made it back in, and a more relieved crew there was not to be found. I was glad that we made it back under our own power, as to be towed in would have taken a lot of confidence out of me.

Building Continues

I continued to build, sail, and read throughout the summer. By fall, I had all the plates tacked on the frames and had learned a bit more about sailing. I had also put up a fence to either hide my project or provide a wind break, I'm not sure which. I was a little embarrassed with this project and knew I would sound like a crackpot trying to explain it to my customers. Luckily for me, my shop is out in the country, so I didn't bother neighbors with my work, and I could kind of hide it for a while.

When winter struck again, I put up some temporary paneling around the base of the upside-down boat hull and started to finish weld all the plates I had tacked in place. When working with steel, you must get all the pieces in place. As the final welding progresses, it is necessary to skip around the hull to keep from drawing the steel too much in one spot, and distort the shape and break temporary tack welds. By spring time, the hull was done, and I was very anxious to see her turned upright. During the winter, as I was working on the boat, I would hang upside down inside and try to imagine what it would be like standing on the quarter deck and looking out over the rest of the deck and over the bow. Gosh, it looked great, even upside down!

In the spring of 1987, I got together a group of neighbors and some interested friends to help with the turning over of the boat. Up till now, it was no problem building it outside as the rain and snow just ran off the hull. When I turned it upright, it would act as a giant bathtub, so the next project would be to make a temporary shed over the hull.

Getting back to the hull righting, the neighbors came (Marion and three of the kids had to be somewhere else that weekend) and with the help of the old drag line, I first lowered down one side and next hooked the cable to the far side and pulled and raised the hull over and up. She looked great, and I was happy with the shape having only seen it upside down before.

My next project was the shelter. I cut down some large poplar trees, put them around the boat, made rafters, and made a roof over the boat. I found some used tin that I made a roof with, and my father-in-law gave me some rough sawn boards to use as walls. This took most of the summer to do, as I was only working part-time on the boat. I was still repairing broken stuff for customers.

By the time winter of '87 had come, I had a hull with a

temporary shelter, but no heat to work with. Next came the forming of deck beams and deck plates. I was anxious to get more of this open hull covered. I left open the area right above the ballast and engine area, as I would lower them down from the top with the drag line. In the meantime, I had been collecting lead ballast for the keel. Lead works the best, as I needed as thin a keel as possible. Using steel or cement would require a fatter keel, so I needed three tons of lead. I had a hard time finding cheap lead till I found 55-gallon drums full of used wheel weights at a tire shop. These I melted down using some home-made bertha torches. I would melt a large ladle holding 500 pounds over a mold and pour it in. It was exciting to be building something this big. The steel molds were made a little smaller than the keel. After the lead had cooled, I hauled them around to the boat, hooked them onto the lift cable on the dragline, and hoisted them to the top of the roof. I had cut a hole in the roof to let the lead pass through. Then I would pour some concrete in the keel first, and as I lowered the three one-ton chunks of lead into the keel one by one, the concrete would flow around the space between the keel and mold. When it solidified it made the lead anchored in place.

I had also purchased a diesel engine that I installed the same way, through the roof. The work progressed slowly because I was only working part-time on it. Also, since everything was done in the boat, it meant that all had to be carried up the ladder, sometimes many times, before it was ready to be welded in place. I was also doing some sailing with the other boat and trying to increase my sailing skills.

In the summer of '87, I organized a trip on Lake Superior with two of my friends, Joe McDonnell and Dale

Hanson, using the *Popeye* boat. They both had some sailing skills, and I thought it would be a great adventure. We trailered the boat from Wannaska in northwest Minnesota, to Grand Marais on the north shore of the lake. We would sail across to Houghton, Michigan, then over to Isle Royale, and back to Grand Marais, planning to take a week doing this. Two of our wives, Marion and Sherry, would drive over to Grand Marais and meet us when we got back. It sounded like a good plan to me; however, we lacked a few sailing skills that we would learn on the trip.

We got to the launching ramp and raised the mast and rigging. This takes some time, and it was late when we left. I hadn't planned to motor much; we're a sailboat, you know, so I only had the five-gallon fuel tank for the engine. We left late, and about ten miles out, there was no wind and some fog. While we were sitting there bobbing up and down and trying to figure out where we were on the chart, no GPS yet, and poor dead reckoning skills; a ship came out of the fog and gave us a great blast on his horn. Instead of trying to scare us, five blasts does that, he was just telling us he would pass us on our starboard side, we later figured out. We never did get our position pin pointed that night, but thought there had to be land to the east; so when the wind came in, we sailed on. The next day we did come on the coast, and by the water tower, we saw we had come short of Houghton and had arrived at Ontonagon, Michigan. At least we hit the right state and entering the river there, we found the first man we met to be a bit of a crab. Later he helped us out by showing us a place to stop for the night.

We spent the next day walking around exploring. It's so different when coming to a new place by boat rather than by car. I'm not sure why that is, but it just feels so much more exciting. The next morning we left and sailed hard for Isle Royale. I hadn't topped off the fuel, big mistake, I was to learn later. About ten miles from Isle we had spotted the lighthouse. We knew from the chart there were rocks all around, so we trimmed the sails to stop the boat and let it head into the waves while we slowly drifted backwards. By morning we sailed and motored into the west or south harbor. We talked to some people on a 38-foot boat that had come over from Duluth that night, and talked about how bad the waves were. We didn't think it was so bad, but then we were just parked and drifting. We spent the day there hiking and sleeping.

The next day we left for the last leg of the trip back to Grand Marais. There wasn't much wind and we used the motor a lot. About five miles from the harbor we ran out of gas, and there was no wind--just flat calm. Rather than call for a tow, we drew straws to see who would row in for gas. I lost. The shore wasn't too far away. We had purposely angled towards it when we knew we would run out of gas. While I was rowing in, our wives had arrived at the dock. Since we weren't there, they had the dock master make a call on VHF to see if we could be in range. Dale and Joe heard the call and said the wives, Marion and Sherry, could be of some assistance to me, if they would drive north of town and look for a man carrying an empty gas can. I had no sooner beached the rowboat and climbed to the highway expecting to thumb into town, when here were Marion and Sherry. They soon had me back with a full tank and I rowed out to the boat. Unfortunately, the current was setting to the north, and I'm sure I had to row extra miles to get back. The engine liked the gas and soon we were heading for the harbor. Then it was everything in reverse and everyone heading home. I learned two good lessons from this trip I'll never forget. Keep a good dead reckoning position, and take extra fuel if there are schedules to be maintained.

Back to boat building. I had found a pen pal who had just completed the same boat I was building, and he was helpful in one major aspect, "this design does float." Since sailboat hulls are such curvy things, it is hard to actually figure out the water they would displace and just where the waterline would be. This is important as a lot of through-hull fittings (holes in the hull) are added to the boat; some must be below the waterline, and some above. Also, the cockpit floor must be higher than the waterline, as all water that collects in the cockpit must be able to freely drain out.

I also met a fellow boat builder, Clink Wilson, who was building a Bruce Roberts 36-foot boat only 250 miles from us. We became very close friends and would talk over our building problems together. Clink and his wife, Ret, spend their winters in the Keys and enjoyed going to garage sales looking for used boat gear. Here in northern Minnesota, one would be hard pressed to find even a used boat cleat, so he would find duplicate hardware and would haul it home for me. Otherwise, I think my entire boat gear came by UPS truck in small boxes.

The following years were spent doing the interior which rapidly shrank as I added galley, navigation station, settee, dinette, head, sink, water tanks, and fuel tanks.

In 1988, I answered an ad in the classified section of a sailing magazine. Someone was looking for a person to help get his boat ready for the cruising season. I told Marion about it, and she thought maybe it would be a good idea for me to get some sailing experience on the ocean. I wrote off a letter and soon got an answer that I could come. The boat was in Puerto Rico, and the owner and I would spend a week or so working on it before sailing over to the Virgin Islands. I could be on the boat for a month.

We actually spent two weeks working on it, due to some rusted line that we had to wait for while it was sent down from the states. It was a good experience. At the time, I couldn't appreciate the stress a boat owner has when you are far from home, but I came to realize it later. The owner of this boat lived in New York. Being crew is a lot different than being owner. Crews go home when the plane flies, but the owner can only leave when all is put away and accounts settled. I did meet a lady sailor, Gizella, who had sailed down from the states on a yacht that was coming down for the cruising season. It had been a rough trip, and she thought she would answer the ad and spend some time in the islands. But she wasn't ready for the work skipper Alex had lined up for us, so she left us at the first port. We kept in touch, and she and I became good friends in later years. She has since bought her own boat and sailed from Boston to the Bahamas one year.

In 1990, we survived a fire that destroyed an old storage building and also started fires in our yard next to the house, in a field, in the woods, and around the boat. Luckily, when there's smoke, there are neighbors coming to help. By the time the fire department arrived from 25 miles away, the neighbors had it under control and only the storage building with some good contents was destroyed.

In 1991, I had the boat pulled out of the shed and around to the other side of my shop. By now it was no secret, and I didn't need a wall or shed to hide it anymore. The main reason for taking it out was to give me more room to get the rigging and mast set up. Also, I thought that since she was going to be spending all of the time outside, it would be good to see how the boat weathered and if the deck had any leaks. I didn't have room to put wheels under the boat, so I devised a system of skids, actually two large poplar trees slid under the cradle. I hired a local farmer with a four-wheel-drive tractor to come pull it out. We got it out of the shed, and that's as far as the tractor would go before spinning. The poplar trees were digging into the ground eight to ten inches and creating too much drag.

I contacted a land developer who had a large dozer to come the next day and hook on. He had no problem pulling the boat till he pulled the end off the log. We reattached the chain and continued pulling. As he got further away from the building, he got up on more solid ground, and the pulling became easier. Soon we had her parked on the north side of the shop. She looked great, a real ocean going sailboat but 2,000 miles from the sea.

A few years before, I had purchased a 50-foot mast, rigging, and winches, so I could weld on necessary pads and attachments. The mast company was in Charlotte, North Carolina, and I could hardly believe their ad when they said free shipping. They were true to their word; and in the month of March, the mast arrived, all 50-feet in one piece. March can be brutal this time of year, and the poor truck driver from Georgia, could not understand just what anyone this far from the ocean would want with so large of a mast. "Did you know something nobody else did?" he had asked me.

Sailing Practice in New Orleans

In 1992, during school Christmas break, we hauled the *Popeye* boat down to New Orleans to check out the area. At that time, we had only 11-year-old Mary and eight-year-old Erin at home. We went through a lot of work for one week of sailing, but it was worth it, as I realized that was where I'd take the boat first. On Lake Pontchartrain in New Orleans, we found a place to launch. It took a while to get it all set up, so we spent the night at the launching ramp. The next day we sailed over to South Shore Marina, and I got a ride back to the truck to bring it back to South Shore parking lot. We sailed into Lake Pontchartrain and through some bridges and canals and back to the marina. It took a few days, and we stopped at a few places to explore. The last day, while in a tight canal with traffic, a white squall came up. I didn't dare go close to shore and get stuck, so I kept motoring in circles to keep from being blown into trouble. Luckily for us it didn't last too long, and soon we were back at the marina.

I think we had more excitement on land than on the water, due to a broken axle on the truck as we were coming home. It was later in the day, before we even left the marina in New Orleans with the boat loaded, and I heard a squeaking noise from the rear axle bearing just as we started to roll. So we had to spend the night in the parking lot sleeping in the boat and camper. The next day, we made it to an auto parts shop where I bought a bearing and replaced the bad one right there in the parking lot.

I believe we had good traveling for about 1,000 miles. About 500 miles from home, at night, near the Twin Cities in Minnesota, the other rear axle broke completely and ejected the whole right wheel, part of the axle, and brake shoes out the back. We felt the jar as the back of the truck fell to the ground and Marion's shout of, "We have fire back there!" made me think the boat had fallen off the trailer. Luckily, we kept everything on the road and ground to a halt off the side of the interstate.

Walking back I expected to see an empty trailer, but the boat looked OK. However, the rear tire and brake shoes on the pickup were gone. We had skidded on the rear axle housing of the pickup making a lot of sparks. That was the fire Marion had seen. We got pulled off the road that night by a wrecker, taking first the boat and then the pickup. I had called Marion's sister who lived about 50 miles away, and her husband, Greg, came for us. We spent the night with them.

The next day, I was able to use one of their cars and found a used axle at a junkyard to replace the broken one, and we were moving again. It was a relief to turn into our driveway after the whirlwind sailing trip. And the poor old pickup, I think I had asked a little too much for it to pull that load so far. That there were easier ways of doing the same thing, there is no doubt; but now that it's over, I can see that it was important to go through this commotion, as it was only a prelude to the events that would happen when we launched the big boat.

A Lucky Break, *Indian Summer* Finds a Ride to the Mississippi River, the Christening and Road Trip

In January of 1993, Marion and I went to Minneapolis, MN to the annual boat show. I usually feel out of place there. It seems like the things I like about boating are not evident at the show. My interests are more in voyaging, not fishing or afternoon sailing. I was mindlessly wandering up and down the aisles, not looking for anything in particular, when I came upon a booth with boat pictures. As looked them over, I realized this was a company that specializes in hauling boats around the country. Now, I had been building my own trailer and had planned to hire someone to pull it for me. When I asked about him hauling my boat, I was amazed that he could do it so reasonably. I made plans for him to come get the boat in the spring, and I stopped building the trailer. Things would move along rapidly now, as there was a deadline to meet. I think Marion was happy to see a plan to get the boat out of here finally. It had been over seven years since I had started it. She was tired of hearing people ask, "How's the boat coming along?" with a smirk in their voice.

Sometimes it seems like major road blocks get thrown up in front of the best laid plans. This summer would be a fine example of that fact.

By spring of 1993, there was a lot more to do on the boat. I hadn't had time to put in the port windows yet, so I just covered them with plywood. I had two fuel tanks aboard, but only one installed, plus many smaller things. The interior takes forever to finish, but the important stuff was done, the boat hull was water tight (I hoped). The steering worked and the engine ran. What else did I really need for the trip down the river? I was learning that when the major items are ready, leave. If you wait for total completion, it might never happen. Life keeps happening and may put a stop to the best of plans. We assigned May 30, 1993, for the boat's Christening Day, as the next day the boat hauler and crane guy would come. We invited many friends and relatives to come. Over 90 people came, and it was exciting to have a little ceremony to give *Indian Summer* her name. I used the christening verse Sterling Hayden used when they christened *Neptune's Car* in the book *Voyage*. *Indian Summer* is my favorite time of year and a time in our married lives together. So, that became her name. After the breaking of the champagne, we all had a good lunch together. Erin had broken the bottle on the first try and no one was killed either, both good omens for boats on christening day. Marion had made a special cake for the occasion too.

The next day my dad, siblings, and some friends came to see the boat loaded on the trailer and helped carry the 50-foot mast to the trailer. My mother had passed away in 1989 or I'm sure she would have been there too. I wonder if she ever thought I'd get it done, as she never said much about it to me.

The boat hauler and crane came at the same time. The boat hauler came from 360 miles away and the crane from 20 miles away. The plan was to hoist up the boat and have the truck/trailer back under it. The crane operator had some spreader bars with canvas belts hooked to them. When he started to lift, the forward strap slid around the bow and let the boat drop with a bang. Not the way to start out. Luckily the boat was only a few inches off the cradle when she dropped, and being steel no damage was done. After tying the straps together the next hoist went smoothly. As the boat sat on the trailer, the boat hauler commented that by the way his trailer was bending in the middle, the boat had to be well over the ten tons I had told him earlier. I sure didn't like to hear that. I was counting on the boat to float at a certain point on the hull. Some openings in the hull have to be above the water. I had kept track of all the metal and gear as I was building and even added one ton for things I had possibly forgot. I could only come up with 10-ton.

After I paid the trucker, I followed him out the two miles to the highway where he stopped to check his load. From his trailer frame to the road, was only three inches. I mentioned this to him and wondered if he would be traveling slower now because of the low clearance. He said, "Jerry, I have found out after years of trucking, you either have no trouble or a lot and traveling slow doesn't help, I like to travel at highway speeds." I don't know if I could agree with him on that, there is a big difference in 45 or 65 in a wreck, but it was out of my hands now. I suppose the load could only drop as far as the highway, three inches, and stop there. I followed him for a few miles in case he did have trouble, but he soon left me at 65 to 70 miles an hour.

The plan was that he would take the boat to the marina near the Twin Cities and off load it, and we would come the next day for the launch. Bay Port is about 350 miles from our home and about the closest point to us, where we could launch and have deep enough water to get to the ocean. We arrived the next day to find *Indian Summer* hanging in the travel lift waiting for us to show up. The trucker had called earlier that day to say the boat was there, and I asked if he had run across any scales on the way down. He hadn't. The weight of the boat was still an unknown factor, a big concern for me now. I really didn't have a plan what to do if it sunk too low in the water; rebuild right there in the marina?

When we got to the marina, I saw scales on the hooks holding up the boat. I asked the operator what the weight was, and he said it was 28,500 pounds. That's 14 ¼-ton! It was over four ton heavier than I had thought. The boat hauler guy knew his trailer alright. Well, it was too late to do anything about it now. As the travel lift moved over the ramps and started to lower the boat in the water, I had this fear that maybe it would not even float. Just before the waterline touched the upper bend or chine of the hull, I felt the boat start to bob. She was floating! And just where my pen pal, John, said it would. Looking in the bilge, I could find no leaks anywhere in the hull or ports. It was a relief for sure! My dad and siblings had come down to see the launch. I had enough excitement for the day and didn't want to even see if the engine would start. My slip was so close that we just pulled it over to it and tied up. I could take only so much excitement and stress in one day.

We spent three days doing trial runs out of the marina getting used to the boat. My sisters and some friends would join us for a short half-hour motoring trip out on the St. Croix River. As cautious as my father was of the water since he had a near-drowning experience when he was young; he even went out on a run with us. I can't say he was relaxed at any time till we tied up at the dock. He knew steel does not float, and we were riding on 14 ¼-ton of it!

It was amazing that things worked so well; no leaks anywhere, the engine ran great, and the steering was excellent! I had designed the steering using a jack-shaft, sprocket, and chain running to a steering sector of a 1961 Mercury station wagon, my own design. It gave me plenty of power on the rudder, and with only three turns lock to lock, it seemed to be about right.

It was so nice to be sleeping on board and finally setting off on the great adventure. I'm glad there was no one there to tell me what problems I could expect to deal with in the future. Ignorance can really be bliss.

After buying some groceries and bidding farewell to family and friends, we motored out and started down the river. We were still in the St. Croix River, and about 20 miles downstream, we motored into the Mississippi River. The beginnings of the Mississippi start way up north, only 100 miles from our home, but it's too shallow for a keel boat like ours. Bay Port is about the northern-most point to put in.

We did have some excitement on the way down. The river was unusually high, and we were able to motor into marinas that normally only had four feet of water but now had 11 feet. Our boat needs six feet, so we had no trouble, except at Dubuque, Iowa. There we cut a corner too close and ran into a sandbank. We were quickly pulled off by a stranger, and the current took us into the marina. In Dubuque, we rented a car and took in some local flea markets, Marion's favorite shopping experience. We even drove over to a town called Galena in Illinois, as it had some pre-Civil War buildings we wanted to see.

Another day was to be a 500-dollar lesson for me in tying off the bitter end of the anchor line. The morning we left a marina the weather was still and very comfortable to be on the water. Later, the wind picked up and since it was coming from the south, it was against the current. This set up a real close chop in the water causing the boat to lift and plunge as we motored into the waves. Suddenly, I heard a ripping metal sound, the steering went dead, and the boat quit moving. I immediately thought it was the chain on the steering jack-shaft that had broken. I called down to Marion to get the emergency tiller, and we slipped that over the rudder post. I gave the engine some more power, and suddenly we were moving. It was steering OK with the tiller, so I waited till evening, after we had anchored to look at the problem. When we came to anchor that evening, Marion went forward to drop the anchor, and it was gone, along with 100 feet of anchor chain. Now I realized what happened, the bouncing we experienced earlier was the anchor falling off the bow of the boat taking the chain with it. I hadn't tied the end well enough, so when I gave the engine more power, the light rope holding the bitter end of the chain, broke. What an expensive lesson!

One of the many interesting things we experienced, was when we had just left a marina and came to another lock and dam a couple of miles down the river. When we radioed for it to be opened, they came back with the information it would be closed for the day for repairs. The current was strong, and I hated to work my way back up river, so I asked if they knew of any place close I could tie to. Well, they didn't, but right after we signed off, the captain of a tug with a group of barges tied to the bank, came on the radio and said we could tie to them if we liked, as he was going to be there waiting too. That was so nice; it was like tying to a floating dock because they were loaded with only three feet above the water. One of his crew came down to help us tie off and said the captain gave him permission to show us around the tug. That was great! The captain was sitting in the wheelhouse when we came up there. You would not guess him to really be the captain. He had cutoffs, long hair, and was kind of scruffy looking. But he was as nice a fellow as you would ever meet. He stayed on the boat for a month at a time, so I imagine it's no use to get all dressed up every day. When the lock was finally repaired and we could go, we wrapped up a bottle of wine with a note for the captain and gave it to one of the crew. As we pulled away, he stepped out of the wheelhouse waving the bottle. What a day for us!

When we got to Portage Des Sioux, we found a marina to keep the boat. We had planned to be on the river only two weeks and one week to get home. I would come back in the fall to take the boat the rest of the way to New Orleans. We rented a car in St. Louis so we could drive back to Minnesota to get our car.

Two weeks later, disaster struck. The levies broke near Portage Des Sioux and flooded all over the area where we had left the boat. The marina had over 40 feet of water in it and they had boat docks tied to the tops of trees. It was a mess! The lady I had met there in Portage, who lived on a houseboat, had agreed to watch my boat. She had left, so I had no idea what had happened to the boat. No one to call, and it was 1,000 miles from home. The marina had no phone for a while, and when they did get one, they wouldn't give me any information on the boat. Later that summer, I did get in touch with the houseboat lady; she had moved back on her boat and reported that my boat looked fine. I made plans to go back to the boat as planned in the fall, and take the boat the rest of the way to New Orleans. I was lucky to find a neighbor boy, Matt McDonnell, who would go with me. He was still in high school, but he had talked the teachers into letting him go. He had to make a video of the trip as an assignment. Joe and Teresa McDonnell, his parents, thought it was alright for him to go too.

When Matt and I drove to Portage that fall, I wasn't expecting to see so much of my boat hull out of the water when we turned the corner at the marina. I saw right away the water level was way below the top chine. That could only mean one of two things, either the boat had lost weight over the summer and got lighter or she was sitting on the bottom. The Army Corps, who controls the dams, in order to drain the water off the fields, had opened them to drain everything down, including the marinas. The houseboat lady had not thought that I had a deep keel under the boat. Houseboats float in just inches of water where I needed six feet. There was nothing I could do but winterize the boat and go home to wait for spring flooding. I paid the winter slip rent, and we drove home. Matt agreed to come with me again in the spring.

Dragging *Indian Summer* out of Portage Des Sioux 1994

When we returned in the spring, the water was only three feet deep but was slowly rising. We were measuring it every day by putting sticks at the water's edge.

Finally, we had four feet of water around the boat. It had stopped going up, but we needed six feet to float. The good news was that the first couple of feet were soft mud, and only three boat lengths back of the boat, we had a good five feet.

The first idea I had was to lash big tractor inner tubes under the boat and try to raise it somewhat to float it into deeper water. I had collected some large inner tubes from a local tire dealer at home. I had also brought along an air compressor to fill the inner tubes. I had talked to a sailor who had done this, and it had worked for him.

We got the tubes under the boat and tied up the best we could. As the tubes were being inflated, they would just slide up the side of the boat. I tried a few times, but our lashings were too weak. Scratch plan A. Plan B was a little more unorthodox. I had rented a sewer pump from a local plumber; and I thought that by sucking a trench out behind the keel of the boat, we could slide it back. I was desperate. The keel itself is only 40 inches deep and eight inches wide; the rest is part of the hull. That means that only two feet of this eight-inch-wide keel is holding us back. I had also brought along a 12-foot duck boat to work in, as we went from side to side of the keel. Well, I think that idea would have had merit too, if the work platform, i.e. duck boat, would have been more stable. The pump worked only too well, and as soon as it got hold of some Mississippi mud, it gave a yank and almost pulled all three of us, Matt, me, and the pump, into the water. I hastily canceled further operations with the pump. I had only one other chance and that was kind of a brute force method. Now, I know I could have hired a big boat to come in and drag us out, but I was concerned about the rudder that would be plowing through the mud backwards. So I didn't want to take a chance on damaging it, besides, I kind of like to do things myself. My third method, was to use 100 feet of cable I had brought along, and stretch it across the water and tie it to a big tree. I had also brought two winches to do the pulling. As I pulled on the cable with the winch, Matt would rock the boat back and forth to break the suction on the keel. Inch by inch we moved. As we moved back slowly, we got into deeper water and the easier it got, till finally we were almost free and in the middle of the marina. The depth was five and a half feet of water, but of course the top layer of mud was very loose. So only about six inches of keel was in that loose mud. We were ready to make a run for the entrance when a guy hollered out from the shore.

He had been watching us and now thought we might like to know there was a cable stretching across our path and laying on the bottom. We soon found the end of the cable and drug it out of our way. Now it was show time, and with the engine warmed up, I pushed the throttle forward. I knew there was a sandbar at the entrance. That was well above our six-foot keel depth, so I needed speed by the time we reached it to bust our way through. We had checked the depth ahead of time and set up stakes to mark the deepest path out of the marina. So as we picked up momentum, I was steering back and forth to stay in the deepest part and close to our stakes. Just as we came to the entrance, I felt the keel drag into the sandbar. The bar hadn't set up hard yet, and with 14-ton and our forward motion, we sliced our way through. It's nice to have solid steel under your feet at times like this. What a great feeling to be on the outside of the marina and in deep water. I made a wide turn out in the river before coming back to the outside quay. We were all smiles and knew that finally, we were going to be on our way!

We finished buying our supplies for the trip and located a spot near the marina where we could leave the car and trailer with a duck boat atop. We only had a couple of locks to move through before we were in the lower Mississippi, then no locks till New Orleans. As we continued south, the river became wider. At the spot where the Ohio River connects to the Mississippi River, we noticed a big change. The lower half of the river didn't have many marinas and no locks, so the current was strong. At times, we would motor through boiling, swirling water and were very conscious that we could be swept over the submerged banks and into a grove of trees, if we didn't keep to the center of the river. In the evenings, we would look for a patch of calm water to tie up in. We never anchored but always tied to something ashore. If we could find an oxbow in the river with an overhanging tree, we would motor up to it and tie to a branch.

One night we were at a loss to find a place to park. Everything was flooded, and we didn't want to trust the anchor in the strong current. There was a Coast Guard tender tied up to some mooring posts, and we inquired about a dock that was supposed to be in the area. They told us it had been washed away, but maybe we could tie up to them for the night. They would check with the Officer of the Day. They gave us permission to tie to them; it was 1994, remember. I don't think they would have let us after the 9/11 attack against the USA. They also told us we could do our laundry and take showers if we wanted. Matt was thinking of joining the Coast Guard after high school, so they enjoyed showing him around. Afterward, he joined them in watching some movies. They told us they had the job of inspecting a given length of the river and making sure the buoys were in its proper place and moving them if required. Sometimes the buoys get damaged or need to be repainted, and that was their job too.

We did make a stop in Memphis, and while there we were invited to a houseboat party. Everyone was so friendly and enjoyed telling us about their travels on the river. They would motor upstream for a few miles and then turn around and coast downstream. I guess it would be a fun way to spend a weekend. Of course, they have parties on them while at the dock. At the marina, there was a shelter with a restored B-17 that was interesting to look over. That was one of the few marinas we stopped at, as there weren't many on the lower Mississippi. A lot of sailors take the Tenn Tom Waterway south by leaving the Mississippi at Cairo, Illinois, going over to Paducah, and then south, by coming out in Mobile Bay. I believe there would be more marinas that way, if that's what a person wants. Since there are more locks there, the current would be easier to work with too.

It took us about two weeks to motor our way to New Orleans. Once in the city, we had to enter a lock to lower us down to Lake Pontchartrain level, then a couple of lift bridges, and we were in the lake. I knew where we were going because of the earlier trip with the *Popeye* boat, to South Shore Marina.

Now I had to locate a marina that had a lift to set the mast. We found one on the other end of the lake. When we got there, the foreman they gave us was a very helpful and a knowledgeable mechanic. All the cables had to be cut to the proper length once the mast was standing up straight. We finished up late in the afternoon, and I decided to get back to our berth five miles away. We left the marina about six o'clock in the evening, and, of course, I didn't think it would be necessary to do much navigating. I should have known better. I asked Matt if he would like to make supper or steer. He chose to steer. I didn't give him a course, as I thought we could easily see the airport located by our marina. While I was below, Matt steered us out away from the shore.

By the time I came up, it had turned dark, and I couldn't recognize any landmarks. I wasn't used to the sudden transition from day to night. At home at the 49th latitude, we seem to get lots of twilight, but here the sun drops fast. I also neglected to figure out a dead reckoning, such as traveling five knots for so long will put you approximately here. So we just kept going till it came to me that we had to be way past the marina. The wind had picked up and since we only had a few cables holding the mast up, the others we planned to attach the next day, the mast was starting to sway quite a bit. We had no charts and no idea where we were except by now I figured we had to be well past the marina. I figured that we had to get closer to the shore to find some landmarks. We knew there was an airport runway that stuck out into the lake. When I spotted an airplane using the runway, I knew exactly where to go. As we got closer, we found the leading lights to the runway. That meant the marina was just before it. So much, much, later than we first thought, we came into the South Shore Marina. It was a relief to be tied up safely again.

These experiences are exactly why it takes so long to become a sailor. We need to go through the fear of being lost and to take better caution next time. Reading about it is not the same thing. We finished the rigging the next day and rented a car to drive back to Portage Des Sioux, our car and trailer rig. It had been a very stressful month; extracting the boat out of the mud, avoiding all the traffic on the last 1000 miles of river, all the problems to sort out in finding a marina to store the boat and get the mast up. I was ready for a break from the stress.

The First Sail on *Indian Summer*

When Matt and I had left the boat that spring of 1994, I hadn't tried to sail the boat yet. So the next trip down to the boat was going to be the test. I had made friends with a Canadian sailor and his wife, and he agreed to come with me on the first time out. Once we got out on Lake Pontchartrain, we shut off the engine and raised the sails. It sure was great to feel the boat begin to move under wind power alone! It was eight years from the time I started building, till I finally got a chance to feel the boat sailing. There was a lot more to do to the boat before I could go voyaging very far, but now I knew that the boat would sail. I knew by now that a lot of boats float, but not all can sail. *Indian Summer* just proved she could sail.

The Canadian sailor had brought his boat down from Canada and had planned to sail to Mexico. Once out on the Gulf of Mexico, his wife got seasick and couldn't get over it, so he had to turn back. I think they just ended up sailing around New Orleans before hauling their boat back home.

The next time I traveled to the boat in March of 1995, Boyd Olmstead agreed to come along. Boyd had some experience in sailing in Minnesota and would be a good crew. Once we got there, I had the boat hauled out to do the boat paint again. There are a lot of critters and scum that hang on the boat hull, and this bottom paint keeps them from sticking and slowing the boat down. Sailboats don't travel very fast even with a clean hull, so every little bit helps. The anti-fouling has to be put on once a year. It took a few days before we got the boat ready to go, and the plan was to take a trip out to the Mississippi Sound. There are four bridges to go through, and three of them are lift bridges. There are a lot of twists and turns, so it's a little stressful the first time out. We made it alright and sailed to Ship Island, south of Biloxi, where we anchored for the night.

The next day we were going to sail over to Biloxi, about ten miles away, but partway there the fog rolled in. Other than the compass, I didn't really know exactly where we were. Boyd had brought along a GPS he had borrowed; but we had trouble figuring out how to use it, and then it quit totally on us. The GPS was just now becoming reasonable in price so regular folks could afford one. It's not good to be drifting around in the sound with fog, shallow water, and tugboat traffic moving through. We figured that by sailing north, we should strike land or hopefully a marker buoy so we could locate our position on the chart. After traveling a short while, we did in fact find a buoy. It was on our chart so we could follow the buoys and compass course into Biloxi and a marina to tie up at. Soon we were walking to a casino looking for a good place to have supper. Later, we returned to our marina in New Orleans, glad to have navigated through our problems without incident. Later on when the GPS units came down further in price, it made navigating a lot easier, but it's still good to have basic navigation skills as a back-up. Electronics tend to fail just when you really need them. I still needed to improve my dead reckoning skills.

Marion Sails for the First Time on *Indian Summer*

During Thanksgiving week, Marion had a couple of days off from her job at school where she worked as a paraprofessional, and flew down to New Orleans. I was already there and met her at the airport. A marina friend had told us of a great restaurant across the lake, and I thought this would be a good adventure. We would sail across the lake, have a good supper, explore the town, and then sail back. A total of 50 miles sailing; easy, you would think. Well, not quite.

We got a late start. During the crossing, it started to rain along with thunder and lightning. It's not wise to be touching metal when it's lightening out so we went below and waited for the thunderstorm to pass. It was dark before we got to the marina entrance across the lake. We were a little turned around, and the shore had too many lights to pick out the red and green marina entrance. This was before I could afford a GPS. I seemed to get lost every time I went sailing. At one point we saw a brighter yellow light. When we shined our flashlight on the sign by it, we saw, "Danger-- Stay Away." We did find the entrance after a while; and as we glided into the harbor, the depth sounder went off telling us we had sailed into some shallow water. We stopped. We were stuck on a mud bank! Now we could see where we should have gone, and the only thing to do was to launch the skiff and set out an anchor to pull us back off the mud bank.

About an hour later we were moving again and found a spot to tie up to. We locked up the boat and walked towards the center of town. It was a nice, warm night for a walk. I was hoping the restaurant would still be open, and it was. We had a delightful meal of shrimp. This would be a reoccurring theme in our future sails. Conditions could go from very bad to pleasant in only a few hours, or from wonderful to panic in seconds. I think patience and preparedness are the key words in sailing. The sail back was uneventful. We had little to no wind to sail with and we left in plenty of time to find the marina before dark. I was learning Seamanship, to plan ahead for arrival time, so as not to try entering a strange area at dark. Marion had a very pleasant stay on the boat and we took in some of her favorite activities such as craft shows, house tours, and shopping. She couldn't take much back with her on the airplane but managed to squeeze a lot of her purchases into the trunk of our car. She had really enjoyed her time on the boat, and I was glad to hear that.

Sailing with Jack and Charlie to the Dry Tortugas

In 1997, I was ready to try a major trip to the Dry Tortugas. They are a group of islands laying 60 miles west of Key West, Florida. I found two eager crew members to accompany me, Jack Davidson and Charlie Viken. Neither of the guys had sailing experience, but what they lacked in experience, they more than made up in willing spirit. This was going to be a challenge in that we first had to get *Indian Summer* hauled out for a sandblast and paint job. I know some people think that to go voyaging you just buy the groceries, fill up with fuel and go. I always have a few jobs to do every time I go, since the boat is so far from home. It's the only chance I have to get things done. Most of the time, it takes me about two weeks to actually leave. Marion says most people have already traveled to the vacation spot, had their vacation, and returned home before we even leave. It's not far from the truth I guess, but why hurry I say. After all, it's an adventure, not a vacation. So I had lots of tools to bring down as we were going to do most of the work ourselves. Charlie had asked why we needed tools, and he would soon find out. The sandblasting I had arranged to have done at a yard close to my boat slip.

I had an old 1973 pickup with a camper on back, which I used to drive a few years ago. It hadn't been driven for a while, but it was always dependable when I did use it, if I didn't haul too heavy a load. It was the same pickup that we had used on the 1992 trip, pulling *Popeye* down to New Orleans, and had all those axle problems. I had the carburetor overhauled and a leak in the rear end fixed. Beyond that, I just changed the oil and filled her up with gas. Charlie drove over to my place and we began the trip from there. We picked Jack up at his home 60 miles south, and we were on our way.

I had fitted the old truck with an extra fuel tank so we made 300 miles before stopping for gas. A routine check of the oil level showed nothing but a bare stick. We had just about run the engine out of oil. Apparently, the seals around the valve stems had rotted and the engine was just sucking the oil out. I started buying oil by the case. The engine purred like a kitten though, no doubt she liked her oil--one quart every 100 miles; 1,700 miles and 17 quarts later, we arrived in New Orleans.

I immediately went to the marina where we were to have the sandblasting done to get a date set up for the job. The sandblaster guy was there doing a project for another boat. He wasn't part of the marina but only came when called. He didn't remember our many phone calls and assurances saying he could do this job, no problem. He reluctantly agreed to do the work. We arrived on the scheduled day and were hauled out and blocked up. I found an address where I could get the marine paint, so drove to get it. It took some time to get the paint and return, as it was some distance away and traffic was heavy.

The sandblasting was to be in progress while I was gone, but when I got back, nothing had been done. Blast man was angry that I had taken so long, and he was having trouble with his help. Actually, the help was having trouble with him. He had turned into a madman and it was even dangerous to get near him. He was throwing blocks around and yelling. We got the boat tented over to contain the dust, and he went to work like a crazy man. I didn't dare go near him till it was done. The ordeal was finally over the next day, and I was glad to be rid of him. The marina owner apologized about him, and I believe they didn't let him work there anymore. We would do the painting ourselves. I like to do as much work as I can myself; that way I don't have to depend on others to get the work done. In the end, we did get the boat painted and launched, and we all found it hard to believe that we were really heading out to sea. The first real sea voyage for *Indian Summer* and her crew was about to begin!

Things went well as we sailed out the Rigolettes and through the Mississippi Sound. I planned to sail straight for the Dry Tortugas. The seas began building as we moved farther from shore. Finally, about 75 miles out, the wind came right on our nose. We were stopped dead. All we could do was wait it out. With the sails down, we rolled from side to side, up and down. We were helpless to go anywhere. In the evening, I noticed a glow to the south of us. It had to be a ship passing. I radioed him to see if he could give us any updates on the weather. It turned out to be a Coast Guard ship, and they informed us that the weather would stay like this for one more day. After the wind blew through, it turned very nice, but calm. We had no choice but to wait for favorable wind.

I was able to make fairly regular ham radio contacts with Bob Carlson giving him our latitude and longitude positions. Bob was an experienced ham operator who lived about forty miles from Wannaska and had agreed to keep in touch with us. He would pass on the information to our wives and friends. One day we had such an exceptional good signal, Bob asked if we would like to make a phone patch to anyone at home. Bob would be able to hook us up to the phone lines. I don't think either Jack or I were able to find anyone at home, so I asked Charlie if there was anyone he would like to try to contact. His wife was at work and he thought she might like a call from him. He did get through, but I think the novelty of a phone call from the middle of the Gulf of Mexico was lost (this was well before mobile phones). She had to get back to work quickly. Well, it was fun to try it out anyway.

Charlie noticed fish swimming around the boat, and we quickly got out the fishing rods. Jack was first to get a strike. It was small, but our fish book showed it safe to eat. Then we saw this colorful fish come by. It was a Dorado. Jack cast out, and the fish was interested in his lure. A few more casts, and he had a fighter on the line. Jack played him for a while to tire him, so he would come close to the boat, and Charlie used the gaff hook. We had two nice fish for supper.

When we finally came to the Tortugas a few days later, it was in the afternoon. On the chart we had, there was a large whiteout in the northwest corner with some chart information in it, but I thought it would still be OK to sail through it. As we got closer to the main island, where the ranger station was, we called them up to say where we were. It was at this time, he told us we were in a reef infested area, and we should turn around immediately and find a buoy on the perimeter. This we should follow around, buoy to buoy, till we came to the southwest entrance. We turned around quickly, and as we motored out, the depth would change from 100-feet to six-feet. Jack and Charlie could see rocks awash near us. It was a tense time till we got clear. We made a wide sweep, and long before we got to the entrance buoys, it had turned dark. We tried to wait it out till dawn, but the current was so strong, we had no idea where we would end up. Finally, I decided to head in for the anchorage off the old Civil War fort, trying to follow the buoys in, I had a GPS by now. We used it to bring us close to the buoys, and then by flashlight we could pinpoint them. We finally made the anchorage, and it was a relief to have the hook down and a chance to relax.

A short time later, we heard voices very near our boat. Upon investigating, we found a neighboring boat had drug her anchor, and it was tangled in ours. We had to lift both anchors up to get them sorted out and reset ours again. By morning, it was blowing pretty well, and our skiff was too small to chance a landing. So we just hung out on the boat till later in the day. Also, the generator on the engine had quit working because we had taken on some water that had soaked the control panel. I made a hasty contact via Morse code as our battery was so low, and I didn't want to drain it down using voice transmission. The maritime net on the ham frequency picked it up and got someone to copy my Morse code. One of my main interests in ham radio was learning Morse code, and even though it was a prerequisite to getting a ham license, most hams have forgotten how to read it. It was fun listening to the ham operators on the maritime net calling out for someone to read my Morse code, and when they did, they would relay the information to Bob. Ham radio is nice when it is working, but too many people think of it as reliable as a phone call. When they don't hear from you on a regular basis, they think the worst. We would sail to Key West and buy some parts to rewire the control panel so the generator would work again and charge our batteries. I had planned to sail right back to New Orleans from the Tortugas, but the damaged wiring and the tropical depression idling just south of Jamaica, changed my mind. We would make a run for Key West.

We did go ashore and look over the old fort. Fort Jefferson is located on one of the islands. The fort was under construction from 1846 to 1875, but never finished. It was one of the largest forts made and protected the deep water anchorage other nations could have used to assault the US. It also was used as a prison during the Civil War, and one of the famous prisoners was Dr. Mudd who treated John Booth's broken leg after he had shot President Lincoln. The fort was later used as a coaling station and was the last stop for the battleship USS Maine in 1898, on its final journey to Cuba.

The 60-mile sail to Key West was terrific. We got an early start and began motoring as there was no wind. As the morning progressed, the wind came in from the north. Soon we had the engine off, and *Indian Summer* was having the best sail of the trip. We came into the anchorage and had a bit of trouble getting the hook to stick because of strong currents. But after a few attempts, we were satisfied that it would hold us through the night. Key West is a high-dollar place. Boat slips run at least three times higher than any previous slip we had been in. Actually, we hadn't been in a slip this trip, either being at sea or anchorage. The advantage of renting a slip is that you don't have to worry about the anchor dragging while ashore. It's a most uncomfortable feeling to not see your boat where you last left her. So in checking prices, we found a slip we could afford if we split the cost three ways. We motored in and tied up.

Clink and Ret Wilson, the Minnesota boat builders I had gotten to know quite well, spend their winters near Key West. They came down to see us and congratulate us on our first real voyage. They came bearing champagne with real champagne glasses. Well, they were plastic but looked mighty real to us. Clink and Ret were a big help to us in gathering groceries and supplies for the return trip home. I found some wire and switches to replace the damaged circuit board while at the dock. Ret had made a delicious key-lime pie, unique to the area, for us. We ate it outside the marina before leaving. The tropical depression was still waiting to make a move, and I'm very grateful to my crew, Jack and Charlie, for staying with the boat. Jack asked Charlie if he was ready to sail. "You bet," was his reply. I was a little worried they would think the Greyhound would be a better way of returning home. It sure would have been easier for them but much harder for me.

We pushed out and headed north and off shore a respectable distance, as shallow water abounds in that area. We made the 130 miles to Pine Island and the Intracoastal Waterway. We motored north in the channels to Tampa before striking out for New Orleans. The first night, we were searching for an anchorage I had found on the chart. It found us before we found it, in the form of a sandbar. We were out of the traffic lane, so we set the anchor, had supper, and went to bed. Things may look better in the morning. Luckily for us, it was low tide when we went aground. By morning, we were floating again.

All the next day, we worked through the channels, and by late afternoon, we were looking for a spot to anchor again. We saw a group of boats anchored near an island so we headed in. Again, the six-foot keel got us in trouble dragging on every bump. Now, on closer inspection, the anchored boats looked rather small and wouldn't need as much water to float in as we did. We veered off and went looking for a channel that showed on the chart. We found it and made our way up to a fuel dock near a fisherman restaurant. Since it was getting dark and they didn't expect any more traffic, we got permission to stay the night if we would be gone by 6:00 in the morning. We walked to the restaurant to eat. We made one more stop near Tampa before clearing out of the Intracoastal channel.

Now we had a straight course for New Orleans. The sailing was fine, a bit brisk, and we were expecting a speedy crossing. Late one night, while Charlie was at the helm, with a proper wind blowing, there was a loud report, followed by a lot of flapping noise, followed by "Jerrrry." Dashing up on deck, I found the halyard, a line that pulls the sail up, had ripped the top of the jib sail clean off. We took down the remaining sail and lashed it to the deck. In the morning, I would fit a spare sail I had brought along. Morning came and immediately it was evident the sail I had brought along had the wrong size hanks. They would not fit over my larger rigging. A jury-rig was needed. So we tied the hanks to the head stay and got the sail up that way. Not real efficient, but it worked. The sail was a genoa from a smaller sailboat, so it was a very light sail for *Indian Summer*. We couldn't keep it up if the wind got too strong. This was a good season for low pressure, i.e. strong northwest winds to develop, and we ran smack into one. We were only 38-miles from Pensacola, Florida and were stopped dead in our tracks, the wind heading us. We were close enough to get regular weather updates from the coast guard. One warning announced, "All boats in the area should seek shelter from the advancing storm. High winds, intense lightening, and numerous water spouts can be expected." Well, we weren't going anywhere and could expect a front row seat, like it or not.

That night the sky was lit up constantly, and at times we did see water spouts. They were correct on the wind too. By morning, we had had enough. I made the decision to run with the wind and waves to Panama City. It's a storm tactic that works well if you have sea room, and we did. The disadvantage was, we were giving up a lot of hard-earned miles and days that we would have to make up to get home. By the time we reached Panama City, 55-miles away, the storm had moved on, or had blown out, and we came in on calm water. There was a band playing and a parade going on. It was all quite a welcoming party for us. It was actually some local celebration, of course. We found a marina for the night and walked uptown for a good supper. It's strange how a day begins and ends. The next day, we motored west through the Intracoastal again. We could only make 40-miles a day. It was prudent to tie up or anchor before dark, because of the channels being so narrow in places and the water so shallow. My impatience to get out of the rough water had added five extra days to our trip.

We mostly motored through the channels and eventually came to the Mobile Ship Channel. We decided to leave the Intracoastal and get back into the Gulf of Mexico. That way, we could sail around the clock instead of shutting down every evening. We were making very good time, as I had the sails balanced and didn't have to steer much. Jack and Charlie were below sleeping. I was standing in the companion way, watching the shore lights of Biloxi, when all of a sudden there was a boat right alongside us. I was startled and thought I had sailed right into another boat. However, it was a Coast Guard cutter that had approached us with her lights off. They had come over to check us out. As they motored alongside us and shined their lights on us, they wanted to know our destination and where we had been. That was all, and they left as quickly as they had come. Charlie and Jack slept right through the incident. We continued on without further problems. By late the following evening, we were motoring into our slip.

The sea adventure was over, and we were all glad to be heading home. On the way home, a major snowstorm came across our path. Only 200 miles from home, the old pickup I was driving skidded through an intersection and struck a car waiting to cross. Luckily, no one was hurt. It was ironic that our major wreck of the trip would be on land, the same as the last trip had been, when pulling the *Popeye* with the same pickup. It would be the last trip the old pickup made to New Orleans, as later I traded it off for some firewood.

We had left home the end of October, and I had told Marion we should be back in Minnesota by Thanksgiving. When sailing, it is very difficult to have a definite schedule. We actually arrived home on December 16. Marion hadn't really minded that I was gone much longer than planned. She was redoing the kitchen completely, and I was spared the mess of the appliances being in the living room. She was cooking in a frying pan in the dining room and was glad I wasn't there so she didn't have to cook for me. What she really minded was that all three older cars that were running when I left had quit running while I was gone. Sometimes she'd had to bum rides to work. Now she was borrowing her parent's car, since they were in Illinois at her brother's place for a few weeks. One car just didn't start because the weather was so cold, and that car didn't have an engine block heater which all cars in northern Minnesota should have. And being I usually do all the car repairs myself, she didn't want to have any of them towed to a repair shop. A used-car salesman had learned of her plight and called to offer his assistance. But she knows I like to pick out cars myself and figured whatever she picked would not be OK with me, so she just thanked him for his concern.

The trip to the Dry Tortugas impressed on me the need for two additions to the boat. One was some type of auto pilot being steering was such a drag. Also, I needed another form of battery charging besides the engine alternator. I bought a Swedish-made, wind-vane-steering auto pilot and began making plans to fit it on *Indian Summer*. This type of steering uses no electric energy and is the auto steering of choice for long distance cruisers because it draws no power from the battery. The downside to it, is your boat has to be well balanced and able to stay on course with minimal wheel movement. It worked well on *Indian Summer*. The wind vane senses the direction of the wind and will keep your boat positioned at the angle you have set by a system of a trailing oar, ropes and pulleys. I brought the unit down to the boat and fitted all the necessary pulleys, ropes, and clutches to the boat. The second item was a wind generator that mounts on a pole at the stern of the boat. However, this item I didn't get till right before our ocean crossing a few years later.

Sailing to Cuba and Back

The next sailing adventure would be to Cuba. This would be the final test for the boat and me. If we both did well on this trip, Norway would be next. I began thinking of crew and thought it would be a great adventure to involve the family in it, if they were interested. Our 16-year-old daughter, Erin, and our grown son, Terry, volunteered to be crew on the Cuban trip.

Since it would be a two-month voyage from the time I left Wannaska till I returned, I knew some of the crew would have to join the boat along the way. Terry was keen to sail the whole distance. Erin, who was still in high school, would fly to Tampa and meet us there. This would shorten the trip for her by a month. As with all best laid plans, they need to be modified. Marion had earned a trip to Spain with her home-party-plan business and had to make a choice between Cuba with us or Spain. She chose to go to Spain, and this made Erin's trip with us questionable. I didn't think she would enjoy the trip if Marion weren't along and told her maybe she better stay home. Erin was sure she would manage just fine traveling to Tampa by herself, and really wanted to join Terry and me to Cuba, so I reconsidered. She could come. Even though I had the wind vane hooked up, it is easier on the crew if there are three or four aboard.

I found another willing crew member in Al Gjerde. Al was so enthusiastic when I first mentioned the trip to him months before we would go. I felt sure he would run out of steam before the trip even started. I need not have worried. Al kept his enthusiasm for the trip right up to and during the voyage. Al would sail with Terry and me to Tampa, actually St. Pete Beach, FL. Then, he would go over to Melbourne, FL, and visit relatives before heading home.

I looked in vain for someone to join Terry and I for the return trip back from St. Pete, after Erin had flown back home. I had mentioned the trip to many people. One person, Roger Anderson, had expressed an interest, but never gave me a positive answer. He did call later, while we were in Florida picking up Erin. He would join us on the way back.

At the start of the trip, Terry and I rode the Greyhound bus to New Orleans from Minnesota. I had left an old car there earlier to drive around once we got to the boat. Al would join us later. As is usual, there is much to be done before the voyage. Terry and I busied ourselves with the projects. Terry is interested in making things aboard safe and easy to use, so he continually comes up with ideas to improve things. Al drove in as planned, but his van was limping badly. Seems the head gasket was blown and was leaking water. The van would never see Minnesota again.

Also, a close relative had passed away and Al was chosen to give a talk at the funeral. Besides, he wanted to be there. He would fly back to Minnesota for the funeral, and then fly back to the boat. If ever he had doubts about the trip, he sure could have backed out then. He never faltered. Terry and I continued the work, and Al left and returned as planned. We shoved off for St. Pete and our connection with Erin in Tampa. We anchored in a small bay on the way out, ran aground, kedged off, all with mosquitoes thick as flies. This time, I thought we would try the Intracoastal Waterway east to Panama City. The winds were against us, and the next night we anchored off a barrier island. The third night, we were close to Mobile Bay. We looked for a quay where we could tie up. We found a long dredged channel that led us into a small fishing harbor. We found a quay to tie up to and got permission to stay there for the night, 20 dollars would do it. We walked up to a nice seafood restaurant for supper. We also thought we would wash up some clothes since a laundromat was available. Now, while the clothes were washing away, a storm warning came over the news. A major storm would descend on us shortly. The little quay we were tied to was going to be a battering ram for our boat soon. We had to move, but where?

In the dark, we sure couldn't go back out that dredged channel. We cast loose the lines and found an open spot, close to the middle of the harbor. There we anchored and waited. We didn't have to wait long. Like a freight train, the wind came threatening to blow us backwards into a large fishing boat tied to a private dock. We were only 20-feet from striking him. To ease pressure on the CQR anchor, I started the engine, and, in the gusts, shifted in gear. The wind left as fast as it came, and a couple of hours later, all was quiet. Here now was a golden opportunity. We could strike our plans of motoring in the Intracoastal Waterway and leave for the Gulf, via the Mobile ship channel. For the next few days, we could expect favorable but strong winds. We could really log in the miles fast, no anchoring every night. We headed out into the Gulf the next morning. It was great sailing! By night the wind had veered to the north, still a good direction for us, and we had a couple of reefs in the sails to keep us up on course.

Al was at the helm and reported a ship closing in on us with lights shining at us. We turned up our radio to see if he was calling. He was. He was a chase boat for a seismograph ship. The ship was dragging a line five miles behind, and we would be cutting directly across it. We were instructed to turn north till he passed. So we dropped the sails and started the engine. Now, we were plunging directly into the advancing waves. We kept this up till we could see the trailing strobe light on the tail end of the line. We were relieved when we could return to our course and raise the sails. Once again the boat picked up the rhythm of the sea.

I didn't have the auto steering hooked up yet and continued to work at it whenever I could. One glorious night, while I was working on it, all of a sudden it began to steer the boat. It was beautiful. I had finally figured out the right combination with the ropes and pulley system. Now the person on watch could walk around the boat checking gear or drop below for a quick sandwich in the galley. It was like having the slave chains thrown off. That night the moon showed a silver path behind us as we steadily sailed southeast. Watching the wind vane steer the boat was amazing! It was always correcting to follow a straight path, much better than any sailor could do. As we neared the coast of Florida, the winds grew light, and finally we had to start the engine and motor toward shore.

As we neared the Florida coast, we stopped for a while to try some fishing. As it turned out, the fish where smarter than we gave them credit for. We caught no fish, but did get in a nice nap. We packed up our gear, started the engine and motored in to the channel leading to Blind Pass Marina. We have friends, Theo and Joyce Griffen, who live aboard their home-built boat, *Stella Maris* at Blind Pass Marina. We were anxious to see them again. They had built their boat in Eagan, Minnesota over a period of ten years. I had traveled down to Eagan to see their boat, a 42-foot-long and 22-ton craft, lifted over their house and set on a semitrailer waiting on their front lawn for the ride to the Mississippi.

We found the marina alright, and a quick call to the harbor master found us a berth for a few days. We got help pulling *Indian Summer* into the tight-fitting slip. It was a friendly place with many live aboards. The boat next to us was named *Popeye*. I was glad to see someone else with my humor.

We had beat Erin by a few days. She was flying in by way of Thief River Falls, Minneapolis, and Tampa. Traveling by sailboat means schedules must have a lot of space in between them. This was OK as we had a lot of tasks to complete before we could leave for Cuba. First on the list, was to get a sticker for the boat. When a U.S. boat leaves the country, it is helpful to have a documented return number. I had previously written to the Coast Guard and received permission to sail in the restricted waters off Florida. The other document needed as of August 1998, was a letter stating that we would be sponsored by a bona fide company or organization. Club Nautical would do this for us, and provide us with a letter stating this, when we arrived in Cuba. We rented a car and used it extensively, driving to the necessary stores and government agency.

Al wanted to stay with the boat for a few days and help complete some of the projects. I was glad of that, as we had plenty to do. While we were at the marina, we did up some laundry. Al had an expensive Gore-Tex outfit that he washed and rather than dry it in a dryer, he hung it up on a bench outside the laundry room. While he was away, the Gore-Tex outfit disappeared. We couldn't believe it. Everyone at the marina was so helpful and kind. Who would take it? Theo was aghast. "No one here would steal it. We leave things out all the time. Where did you leave it?" he asked. When Al showed him the spot, Theo immediately knew what had happened. The exact spot Al had laid his suit to dry was the "give away spot." Theo explained that when people at the marina want to give things away, they leave it there, kind of a recycle spot. Al immediately put up a wanted poster for his suit on the office door explaining his ignorance of the "give away spot." It was returned as soon as the mistake was realized. Al was happy.

We hooked up another set of running lights, installed life-line webbing, hung additional cabin lights, and finished up the necessary paperwork. Finally, it was time for Al to leave. We drove him across Florida to his relatives in Melbourne. Erin would be in Tampa soon.

We drove to the airport on the afternoon Erin was to land. We had gotten there in plenty of time and were waiting for the flight to come in, when we heard my name being paged. Who knew we were there? I picked up the phone and it was my daughter, Sara. Erin's flight had been delayed, and they had rerouted her to Detroit, so she would be in on a later flight. Terry and I left for a while and returned to pick up Erin at the new time. Things went as planned this time, and we drove back to the boat without further problems. The next day we drove to Bradenton, not too far away, to visit with Marion's aunt and uncle, Bea and Evan Grahn. We then bought our groceries for the next few weeks and returned our rental car. One piece of advice we had received from Theo, was to have soft drinks and cookies or sandwiches ready for the Cuban officials. It never hurts to start out on a friendly note. Theo had been there a few times before.

We sailed out, and once out in the gulf, found very light winds. I didn't want to use up our fuel supply getting to Cuba, feeling it would be put to better use on the return trip. It became a trend on the outbound leg, to drift during the day and sail during the evening when the wind would come in, probably due to the offshore winds that develop when the sun goes down. Terry and Erin would swim during these afternoon calms.

Erin also had homework that her teachers had given her to work on while she would be gone. She would be gone longer than the established time allowed and would actually be dropped from the school roster for a few days. The school would lose some revenue because of this, but I think they saw this as a golden opportunity, for her to learn something firsthand about a country not normally visited by U.S. citizens.

As we neared the coast of Cuba, we raised our courtesy flag and the quarantine flag on the starboard spreader. This meant we had not cleared customs yet. Also, we proudly flew our America flag from the stern. I started calling the harbor master at Marina Hemingway about 15 miles out. The marina where we would stay was seven miles from Havana. Havana has a good harbor, but no facilities for a small boat clearing in to the country. We received no reply as we sailed closer to the coast calling every 15 minutes. About seven miles out, we received a hurried call from shore asking if we were the blue sailboat approaching and what our intentions were. "We have come to visit," was my reply. "Welcome to Cuba!" was their reply. Then we were asked if we had ever been to Cuba before. "No." "Then you must follow my precise instructions to enter." He gave us compass coordinates to come in on. Then he told us to turn sharply to our left once we had cleared the last marker, and come to the dock where officials would be waiting to clear us in.

There is a reef lying near the shore through which we must pass. The ocean depths rise up sharply and give no warning of the approaching rocks. Through this reef, there is a path we must follow indicated by the range markers on shore. There is a mean current trying to drag you sideways into the rocks as you attempt this passage. We came through the passage alright, compensating for the current, found the dock with waiting officials, and tied up. After six days from leaving St. Pete. Beach we had arrived!

First to come aboard was the doctor, complete with

white coat and briefcase. As Terry and Erin stood on the quarter deck, the doc and I went below to do the necessary paperwork. First he introduced himself and welcomed us to Cuba. Then he asked to see our toilet. In there, he raised the lid and sprayed a bug killer. He looked over our passports and made note that we all appeared healthy. Then he asked our last port of call and date. When I said, St. Pete Beach, he was confused.

That was six days ago. 260-miles for 6 days, rounds out to about 43-miles per day, surely we had stopped somewhere else. He wasn't convinced till I pulled down our chart and showed our day-by-day progress. We were advised then, that we could lower our yellow quarantine flag, but to remain at the dock, as more officials would want to see us.

We were boarded by agriculture; they looked over our food stores, taking interest in the home-canned venison I had brought from home. Also, while looking me straight in the eye, I was asked to give up any eggs we had aboard. We had none, and our lack of eye blink at the crucial moment, convinced her I was telling the truth. Cuba is protecting her poultry population by keeping anything that might bring in any disease. The Coast Guard wanted to know if we had guns aboard; customs people, if we had any trade items that we intended to leave. None on both counts. Also, commenting that I had a very beautiful daughter, I thought that was nice, we think so too, I had said. Most officials gladly accepted a soft drink when I offered it. Finally, we were cleared to go to the assigned dock.

About four officials were heading that way too, and they asked if they could ride along. I was glad they would be along to help me find the right spot. We pulled away from the quay and headed to our berth for the next few days. Pulling into the dock area, we found the slip and secured the lines. I couldn't believe we actually were here! The officials left and we were on our own to explore the area. I sent Terry and Erin to reconnoiter the marina; I was content to be left alone on *Indian Summer* and relax for a short time. No more decisions to make. This is a time I like to coil lines and straighten up gear. It's a winding-down time for me just doing things that didn't take any thought. The kids returned later with a general layout memorized. It was nice to know what we had available to us here.

Next item, was to find a phone and call Marion to let her know we had arrived safely. I know she would be worrying till she got a call from us. We had been making regular ham radio calls back to Minnesota via a ham friend in Pennsylvania. Now in Cuba, I had no authorization to use the radio, so we had to resort to the regular phone. We found a phone in the lobby of a nearby hotel. The desk clerk made the call. I had been warned that a phone call from Cuba would be expensive, so the kids were instructed to make the conversations quick. Well, they were quick by normal standards and by nine minutes and 40 dollars later, we hung up. Marion was relieved to hear from us, and I was glad she knew we were OK. Now, we would attempt to find a way into Havana, an adventure I had been looking forward to for over a year.

That afternoon, I was exploring the area around the marina when a Cuban came up to me and started a conversation. He had noticed my Leatherman knife I always carry on my belt. He had one similar. He asked if I was looking for a taxi. Not now, I replied, but tomorrow we would be looking for a way into Havana. He owned a taxi and would be happy to take us. We arranged a time to meet. Returning back to the boat, I told the kids that tomorrow we would be touring Havana. We were excited!

The next day, we met the taxi as arranged. We left the marina, and as we motored into the city, we noticed people on all forms of transportation: bicycles, a horse-drawn trailer, homemade scooters, a lot of motorcycles with side cars, trucks loaded with passengers, plus the normal buses and older cars. Hitchhiking seemed very common and acceptable. A group of people would be waiting on a street corner. When a car would stop for a light or stop sign, the people on the corner would motion for a ride. It looked like most drivers would accommodate them. Even motorcycle riders were asked for a ride.

And, yes, there were the early fifties autos too. Terry and Erin tired early on, from my astonished reaction to seeing so many of the Fords and Chevys of my younger days, still being used. Even though they seemed to lack the roar of the flathead 239, or 256 V/8 engines, they still reminded me of high school days and all the time spent working on those cars. The pollution was noticeable.

We saw some of the important buildings in Havana and the harbor leading into Havana, with the battleship Maine memorial which was paid for by the people of Cuba in appreciation to the US for freeing them from Spain. On the memorial were salvaged guns and anchor chains from the ship.

The streets were clean and things looked orderly. After the drive around Havana, we stopped at our driver's house to meet his wife and see his place. It was an apartment on the ground floor, very clean and comfortable. We met his wife, a petite lady. She disappeared into the kitchen to make us coffee. Rumaro took us outside to show us their bedroom. We climbed up a ladder on the outside of the house through a cutout in the eaves. There on top of the roof was another small room. I could see why it was a good place to sleep, as it was high enough to catch some breeze. Laundry also swung from clothes lines. Around the perimeter was broken glass set in concrete to discourage anyone from coming onto the roof by any other way.

Then Rumaro took us to meet some more of his relatives: grandparents, aunts, uncles, and cousins. When Terry, Erin, and I came in the living room, we had three chairs set out for us. The relatives, about eight or ten of them, gathered around and began showing us pictures of their families. We were served Cuban coffee. It was a shame that only Rumero could speak English, and not too fluently either, but I hasten to say much better than my Spanish. We wished we could have understood what they were telling us about their families, of which they were obviously very proud. I had the feeling Rumero was a little proud to be showing us around too, and we were so glad he took the time to do it.

The next trip into Havana, we wanted to see Hemingway's home. We were taken through the city, and when we got to his home, it was closed for the day. We did get a picture by the gate and got a chance to see inside the fence. After that, we got a tour outside the city. There seemed to be rather large hills we were driving through. There was some language difficulty between Rumero and us, so we missed some of his explanations. On the way back to the boat, we stopped at his parents' house and met his mother and sister.

The next day, we hiked around the outside of the marina. We noticed that most areas were very clean and no garbage was being blown around. One time we were stopped by a man waiting with a group for a bus. He asked where we were from. Then he told us about his relatives in New York. He explained that he liked to practice his English whenever he could.

We were now confident we could survive a hiking trip in Havana, so we arranged to be dropped off and picked up near the downtown area. Rumero was to pick us up in a few hours. He wrote on a piece of paper, "Be Careful."

We hiked towards the Havana harbor on the Malicom main drag. The Malicom is a major boulevard running along the sea. We stopped to watch some fisherman and got a picture of a puffin fish he caught. He poked it with a stick, and it puffed up. We got to the harbor entrance, and the view was wonderful! A group of school kids were taking turns jumping off the quay into the sea. A tall jump, it looked dangerous. This was the harbor the battleship Maine was anchored in when she blew up and started the Spanish-America war.

We continued towards the center of town and couldn't help noticing how clean things were. This takes a conscious effort to maintain. We had a hard time trying to figure out what was sold in the stores, as there seemed to be a lack of advertisement signs on the outside of the buildings. We returned to the spot where Rumero would pick us up. There were some kids playing soccer, and they talked Terry into playing with them. After the game, they asked me for a dollar each. This was the only time we were hit up for money. That they were the first and only ones to do so, I was impressed. I did give them something, but Terry thought I should have been more generous. I guess he could have given them something, if he felt like it.

At the marina, we met a couple from Minnesota and a couple from Canada. The rest of the people we met were mostly from European countries such as France and Germany.

I had been working on a stencil to use on the quay we had tied to while in Cuba. I wanted to leave a mark in the cement saying we had been there. The day before we left, Erin volunteered to paint it on the dock. Rumaro and another Cuban sat down on the dock with her, and helped her paint it on the dock.

On the day of our departure, there was a storm passing through. The seas kicked up quite a fury, and we were happy to still be in port. We had allowed for plenty of cushion time and were in no hurry to leave. Our only real schedule was Erin's flight back to Minnesota from Tampa. We waited two days before clearing out. We had to leave our marina quay and motor over to the clearing out dock. When we were ready to push off from the dock, a group of Cubans that we had come to know while we were there came to see us off. We got a group picture of all before leaving. I couldn't help wonder what they were thinking. Maybe they were thinking it would be nice to be able to be sailing out too.

We got to the clearing out dock and were boarded by Coast Guard officials. The paperwork was minimal. Once the inspections were done, we were under surveillance till we motored away from the dock. Only those arriving onboard are permitted to leave. Once we got outside, the seas were very lumpy, and there was no real wind to drive us. The waves kept throwing us around, and at times we found ourselves sailing back toward Cuba. We had cleared out around noon, and we sailed the rest of that day and the next day. By midnight, we were motoring into the Dry Tortugas.

We needed a break, and this was the first chance to put the hook down. It was very dark when we came into the channel leading up to the Civil War fort. Twisting back and forth, we wound our way to the anchorage. When we got there, much to our dismay, we ran aground and badly. The more we twisted and turned the worse it got. We were on a falling tide. "Well, the only thing we can do is go to bed," I said. "Let's see what it looks like in the morning."

When the sun came up, I knew things were not good. I could feel the boat heeled over more than it ever had before. A look outside made me cringe, there wasn't three-feet of water around the boat. We needed six-feet to float. I had never laid over this far before, and I didn't know if the boat would right herself before flooding the insides. Some boats will fill with water and flood before they get a chance to get upright. I'm sure a few pictures were taken of us that morning as there were a lot of other boats around. We were the entertainment for the day, I guess. I couldn't bear to even take a picture. It hurt too much to see the boat like that.

The wind picked up some speed as the morning grew. We were asked if we needed a tow by a departing fishing boat, but I declined. I thought there would be too much damage done while we were still laying over that much. As the tide came back, the boat began to rise up. Hooray! We raised the sails in hopes of being blown off the sandbar. No luck. We set out the anchor and cranked hard on the winch. No luck. We ran the engine and turned the rudder back and forth to try wiggle off. No luck. The ranger came out to offer assistance, and he hooked onto us and was able to turn us so we faced downwind. We could get no farther. By this time, it was a half-hour to high tide, and we were still just bumping, but not floating. There would be very little water rise now. The future looked bleak, and we may spend another tide cycle lying down again.

Then, two rubber rafts came up to offer assistance. They were from some anchored boats nearby. They hooked their boats in tandem and took our main halyard out to the side. Terry and another man hung out on the boom while Erin and one of the ladies cranked hard on the winch that was hooked to the anchor. I ran the engine, and all together with the sails drawing, we slid off the bank into deep water. What a relief! It was a good lesson to keep in mind, that by pulling on the halyard attached at the top of the mast, you get a 50-foot lever to pull the boat over and reduce the amount of water needed to float.

After we anchored in deeper water this time, we went ashore and looked over the fort. I had been there once before with Jack and Charlie. Terry and Erin swam around the island. By evening, we were back aboard and after listening to the weather forecast, it seemed like a good idea to shove off that night. The wind was very light and we motored most of the night. The North Star showed bright. All we had to do was keep it to one side of the mast and we would be heading due north. We got into St. Pete. Beach and I called customs to report our return to the country. We rented a car again and got Erin to the airport for her return trip home. We also picked up Roger Anderson who would sail with Terry and I, back to New Orleans.

As we prepared for the trip across the gulf, Tampa to New Orleans, a distance of over 300 miles, we watched the low pressure systems come across from northwest. There were only three days between them at times and with the slow speed of a sailboat, I knew we had to weather at least one of them. We picked a fine day for our departure, and left with the sun shining and a light breeze blowing. Soon the wind fell and we motored. Roger was doing fine and we all hoped for the best.

On the beginning of the third day out, on Roger's watch, it was 2:00 a.m.; the wind came in like a fury. I was helping Roger keep us on course, but the wind was changing direction so much, or else the boat was being thrown off course, that the sails would not stay filled. As a result, they would whip violently, and it would be only a short time before they would rip, so we took all sails down. *Indian Summer* rolls somewhat with no sail on and a sea running, but until we got breaking seas, the deck stays dry. It was time to go below and wait it out.

Terry was sitting at the table, braced against the compression post to keep from being thrown around, and when Roger and I came down, he asked why. I said we had lost interest in sailing for a while. The wind was against us and the seas were building. Down below the motion was a bit rough, but drier. We still had to keep watches, even though we weren't moving. Ships can still plow through these seas and we would be hard to see in these conditions.

The waves built through the night, and by morning they were impressive.

Roger had never experienced these conditions before, and was getting a bit seasick, plus he was trying to sleep in the vee bunk. There was a lot of motion up there. Terry and I already had our sea legs, so we were fine. At present, we were in no danger, lots of sea room and everyone still aboard. We would just wait it out. We set the sea anchor, a large parachute that is streamed from the bow on 400-feet of 5/8th-nylon line. This is designed to keep the bow a bit more to the waves, thus keeping the rolling motion to a minimum. We didn't have as much free board and windage, so the wind force on us was reduced. This helps in some ways, but without this force *Indian Summer* sails back and forth on the end of the line. The storm anchor did help though and it reduced our rolling some. When Roger got up, he spent some time in the cockpit munching on crackers and trying to get his sea legs too.

By evening, the wind had clocked around to the NE and we were able to pick up the storm anchor and began sailing again. Soon we were crashing along with the spray flying, and we were right on our course, all was fine. There was another low coming down that would again turn the wind against us before we got to the Mississippi Sound, so we changed our course to Pensacola, a closer port. It would be a race to see if we could get in before the low hit. We made it and found a nice harbor to tie up in, complete with a restaurant. It was good to be in port while the wind howled. We spent the day there.

When we left, we motored through the Intracoastal Waterway with complete protection from the unsettled seas.

As we neared Lake Pontchartrain, there are a number of bridges that must be opened. The procedure is to call ahead to the bridge tender to open it for you. At the first bridge, we radioed for a bridge opening and with the engine in neutral we drifted towards the bridge. However, it was not going to open completely before we got there. The wind was from behind and we were drifting a bit too fast. I put the transmission in reverse. There was a strange clunk that I hadn't heard before. We didn't seem to slow down, even with the engine in reverse, but the bridge opened soon enough for us. When it was clear I put the transmission in forward and revved up. Nothing happened. The wind was still blowing from behind, so we drifted on through. Once through the bridge, I quickly jumped below to check out the problem.

A big problem had surfaced. The coupler that hooks the engine to the transmission had broken. We had no auxiliary power now. Terry suggested that we try sail as far as we could since the wind was in our favor. We hoisted the sails and in the process ran aground on a sandbank. The wind had increased enough, that we heeled over and slid off the bank into deeper water. We had no problem sailing the channel back to the lake, we had another bridge to go through and it would be a new experience for me to sail through. This bridge had a break in the middle with hinges on each end. However, for some reason, the bridge tender only opened one side. It looked tight, with our mast 50-feet we stuck up way beyond the bridge. I kept my speed up to provide good steerage and we cruised right on through, no brakes. We made it all the way to the bayou entrance and into the bayou. I couldn't believe our luck! Maybe we could sail right to the marina?

The waterway wound back and forth and finally ½-mile from the marina we headed right into the wind and stopped. That was as far as we could go. It was getting late in the evening and I thought it would be good to wait till morning to go for a tow. Roger was anxious to get something lined up that night, so I decided to launch the skiff and go to the marina to check for a tow. I got to the marina and found the caretakers. They agreed to come get us in the morning. I motored back to the boat in our noisy outboard. We were aground lightly on the bank of the bayou and I figured it was going to stay that way, so didn't put out an anchor. With everything seemingly under control, I thought supper would be in order. While we were lollygagging below, we heard voices in a boat close by commenting about a boat with no lights. On coming up on deck, I saw we had drifted off the bank and floated across to the other bank. I still had things to learn about rising tides and keeping boats lit at night.

I set out an anchor this time, before we went to bed and lit the lantern. In the morning our tow came as planned. Finally, we would be in our dock, adventure over.

Well, not quite, there was more adventure coming. In the towing effort, the towboat had run into a mud bank and plugged the water intake. Their engine began to overheat. It was a borrowed boat and they lost all interest in further towing. Now, it was my time to tow them back to the marina in the skiff. It seems like the only operating boat was our little 8-foot skiff. Back to the marina we came, straining, jumping, and lurching to tow the towboat. When they were safely at their dock, they started to work on cleaning out the water intake and filter. I motored over to a boat repair facility. There a customer accepted the challenge to tow us in. This went ahead without a hitch and we were towed into our slip and finally tied up. I felt like a huge weight had been lifted off my shoulders. We spent the next day closing down *Indian Summer*. The drive back to Minnesota was uneventful, thank God, I couldn't stand much more!

The Cuban trip had proved successful in exposing some weakness in the boat. One was the coupler and second we noticed that the bottom paint had failed. The coupler was just a matter of installing a new one. The transmission was also acting up. It would not shift into gear sometimes unless it was revved up. This is very inconvenient when maneuvering in tight quarters, like in a marina around many boats. Forward and reverse being your only way of controlling a drifting boat. Another work expedition would have to be organized, before I could sail to Norway

Re-Sandblasting the Hull in New Orleans

In the fall of 1999, Keith Severson and I were driving back down to the boat from Minnesota. Keith was a student and expressed an interest in coming with me sometime. He agreed to help me work on the boat. This was going to be a marathon job, as I didn't want to repeat the bad experience I had last time, with the crazy sandblast man. I would do the job myself, that way I knew what to expect. We headed down to New Orleans in my welding truck, pulling a small trailer with a 400 Kawasaki motorcycle that I would leave with the boat. I was hoping that I could find room for it onboard when we sailed for Norway.

On arriving at the boat we located a sandblast rental

place and a supplier for sand. The marina where we had contracted the last sandblast job, had told me over the phone that they wouldn't let me blast there, so I was preparing to sail across the lake to a more commercial haul out facility. As a last ditch effort, I talked to the owner of the closer marina to see if there would be any way I could use his facility for the job. He relented and said only that I must tent over the boat while blasting. Also, if he was going to paint other boats, I would have to stop for the day. This was agreeable to me, so we motored over and began gathering the necessary equipment.

I rented a portable welder also, as I was going to get rid of the silly life lines for some serious one inch pipe. If our lives needed to depend on them, I wanted them strong and ridged. We began sandblasting and the bottom paint stripped off very easily. We got the bottom painted before the evening dew came in. The next day we stripped off the top side paint. It was getting late when the last paint was applied. I kept the tarp over the hull in hopes that the dew wouldn't affect the paint and keep it from bonding to the steel. We had rented the equipment over the weekend, and Monday I would have to have it returned. We still had the railings to weld in place, so very early Monday morning I got up and began welding. Soon, I found the marina owner standing next to my boat. He had been called down by the police who had received a report of sparks and fire at his marina. Of course it was only me welding, but it did give him a panic attack. I was sorry for the concern I had caused and realized then how serious it must have looked from the highway. We had used up three-ton of sand and our backs felt it. It was a good job to have done, *Indian Summer* looked sharp, black with a white deck. It was worth all the effort.

When we got the boat back in the water we still had a few days before we had to start for home, so I felt we needed a short cruise. We would go to the north end of the lake, through the causeway. I had never been there before. We would tow the skiff behind. The wind was perfect, about 12 knots from the beam. Keith wanted to try out the skiff, he had run it before around the marina and I felt he could run it safely. The motor was greatly overpowered for the craft at 10hp, but if the operator would sit farther forward than usual, and only run the engine at half throttle, all would be OK.

Keith boarded the boat and pushed off, I continued to sail as he had no trouble keeping up with me. After a while he came in and I handed him a camera to take pictures of me under sail, I had no pictures to date of the boat actually sailing, it would be nice. This he accomplished alright, and he came over and handed me the camera. Next, he would come from behind and tie to the stern. I had kept sail on, as it would take too much time to stop, and it was getting late for our arrival at the dock. With the skiff tied to the stern, and me sailing about four knots, Keith made a jump for the stern, missed a handhold and fell into the lake. The skiff ran over him breaking the tow line. He was in no danger as he had a life jacket on, but the water was cold. I got the sails down and turned the boat around. He climbed aboard and we began trying to drag the skiff and outboard motor aboard. We didn't have enough strength to do it. I disconnected the motor from the transom, having first tied it to the railing. We hoisted the dripping motor into the cockpit. The skiff was a bit more of a challenge, but we persevered and eventually got it aboard too. Keith was getting cold and he went below to change.

It was dark when we came into the town on the north edge of the lake. We found a nice place to tie up and walked to a restaurant for supper. Later, I would find a water hose and flush out as much of the engine as I could. On the way home, just before coming into the bayou, we hooked a crab trap and had to free ourselves from it. This meant going into the water to untangle the line from us. I was getting ready to do this when Keith volunteered. He felt that he was getting more used to the water than me on this trip, I relented. We came to rest at the home slip and closed up the boat.

Before leaving though, I removed the transmission and took it to a repair shop, as it was still slow to shift into gear. Also, the main sail was dropped off at a canvas shop to put in a third-reef grommet. There would be many pieces to come together at a crucial time when we sailed for Norway. The drive home was tiring but uneventful, the best kind.

Gathering Crew for Norway

Back in Minnesota, there were many things to put together. I still needed to pin down the crew. I had spoken to Terry in September, and he had expressed a desire to sail with me. I would have wanted to add another member to the crew, but it's hard to find someone willing to take an entire summer off for the voyage. I was resigned to sailing shorthanded, if we went at all.

In early winter, I applied for a factory job at a town nearby. They were advertising for workers and I was on the fence as to whether I wanted to continue my welding business. Probably, I was subconsciously trying to find a good excess for not going. I figured that if Terry would back out on the trip, I wouldn't go. I had a lot of pre-planning done and was not just idling along waiting for spring. The factory had accepted me a few months later and I started work in March 2000. I was not sure I would sail.

Then things began to happen. Mary, our daughter in college at the time, mentioned to a group of friends that her dad and brother were thinking of sailing to Norway. One of her friends was very interested in the trip and told her to tell me he would like to join us. Ben had no sailing experience and had never been on a sailboat before. His interest in Norway, came from his ancestors and he was studying the language. When Mary told me about Ben's wish to sail with us, she didn't know if he was serious. She would have him e-mail me if he was really interested. Soon I received an e-mail from him. He was interested, and would like to join us in Bermuda when we stopped there to resupply.

Now another potential crew member showed up. Stuart Mickelson from a neighboring town indicated that he would like to sail with us too. He didn't have all summer, but could be gone from work for two weeks. This would help Terry and me in our sail to Florida. I figured a few days to ready the boat; a week to sail to Florida, and Stuart would have time to get back home.

I had talked Ben into joining us in Florida and sailing to Bermuda. Then, if he didn't like it, he would be free to leave. The problem with starting from Bermuda, would be the Gulf Stream and westerly winds. It would be very hard, if not impossible to turn around once leaving Bermuda, if he couldn't adapt to sailing life. I needn't have worried, Ben turned out to be an excellent sailor. Now things were beginning to snowball.

I was approached by another friend, a former crew member, Roger who wanted to be in on the trip too. He would like to join Ben in Florida and sail with us to Bermuda. Now I had the crew, I was committed to going. I quit the factory job after only six weeks. I hadn't even gotten tired of the job yet, but I needed to get a lot of things in order for the trip.

The trip to Cuba showed me that our battery charging system needed some help. The only way we had of charging the batteries was with the engine alternator. If we lost that, we had no backup to charge them. I found a wind generator that would help us keep the batteries charged.

I had taken the outboard engine home to work on it after its swim in the lake, as I couldn't find anyone in New Orleans that would do the work. I also had an extra water tank and navigation books to bring down to the boat. Since I planned to take the bus down to the boat, I needed to ship a large box with all these items in. This was beginning to take on a real expedition atmosphere. I loaded the box with all these items; outboard motor, wind generator, engine coupler, navigation books and anything I needed that wouldn't fit in my duffel bag. This big box I hauled to a local trucking company that would get it shipped to New Orleans, and over to Slidell, Louisiana, where the boat was now. A neighbor, Steve Reynolds, wanted to come to New Orleans and help us ready the boat for the trip. Marion would drive Steve and I to Fargo, our bus would leave late in the evening. May 5th would be the day we would leave Wannaska for Fargo, and board the Greyhound bus for New Orleans. Stuart would meet me there, and Terry would meet us in Minneapolis, as that was his home. I estimated that a week would do it for Steve.

2000 The Trip to Norway Begins

As we drove south out of Wannaska, I couldn't help reflecting on our latitude position and the next time we would see 48 degrees 33 minutes latitude, we would be in the north Atlantic. Marion had just come home from a trip overseas and had twisted her back. She was in a lot of pain, and I wished there would have been another way to get Steve and me to Fargo, but it was too late to change now.

The ride to Fargo was quiet and we were all deep in our thoughts. I could only imagine what the others were thinking. I knew Marion was not very happy about this. Steve, maybe wondering what he had agreed to, and I was thinking of all the things that could go wrong. Too many pieces have to fit together to make this project work. I always hate goodbyes and a lot of water would pass between us, before we would see each other again.

I had arranged a ham radio contact man, Bill Landby, who lives in Warroad, Stuart's town, and we would try making regular contacts. I didn't know how well this would work the farther we got out in the ocean. We used the ham radio on our two trips across the Gulf of Mexico. When radio conditions deteriorate, people ashore get concerned when they don't hear regular reports. Sometimes I think it's not good to have too ridged a schedule.

When we got to Fargo, we stopped in front of the bus station. We unloaded the bags and Marion and I hugged for a

77

while. How can one be happy and sad at the same time? I wished she was going with, but knew the voyage would be too hard on her and our relationship. She would meet us in the Shetland Islands, and sail the last 200 miles to Norway with us. We kissed and parted. Stuart came in a few minutes before we boarded, he had ridden the bus from Grand Forks, and was visiting relatives during the layover. We left Fargo bound for Minneapolis.

We arrived in Minneapolis early in the morning. We had a layover there. One of our daughters, Mary would take Terry to the bus station and also bring Ben along, so I could meet him firsthand. I had yet to see him, our only contact being through e-mail. They arrived on time and it was good to finally meet Ben in person. Terry had discovered that he had left a crucial piece of gear in his locker at home, his bus ticket. There was no time to return for it as the bus was leaving shortly. He would have to take a later bus and meet up with us in Chicago. We boarded the bus and left for Chicago.

During one of the rest stops we actually saw Terry walking around, as our bus pulled out, he must have gotten an express bus. In Chicago we were all united. We got to New Orleans and then to Slidell, late in the afternoon, total bus ride of 40 hours. We unloaded the boat of all the storage gear, and set up the tent I had used as a warehouse in previous trips.

Steve had his choice of sleeping on the boat or in the tent. He chose the tent unaware that there are alligators roaming the area at night. Maybe it was good he didn't know. I'll bet he slept better that way. This fact about the alligators, we found out later.

We had a lot of work to do and many things had to click right the first time. We had schedules that required people to be gone only a certain amount of time. Not a good thing when dealing with sailboats and unpredictable wind conditions. We got the transmission back from the repair shop and installed. Also, the new coupler was bigger than the old one, so I had to hacksaw out part of the boat frame to make it fit. The box had arrived and was delivered to the boat. We got the wind generator out, and located aluminum to make a stand for it on the stern. We repainted the deck, cleaned out the fuel tanks, collected the main sail from the sail maker, and inspected the boat from top to bottom.

The day before Steve was to leave, I declared it a holiday and I rented a car so we could see some of the sites. We saw the battle ground of the Battle of New Orleans 1814, and the French Quarter. Steve had a sister that lived close by, so we dropped in on her also. The next day I took Steve to the bus and went to the clinic to pick up Terry. He had been bitten by a dog and we were concerned about rabies. The dog and Terry checked out alright. With departure day approaching a lot of possibly delays where being thrown in our path.

Finally, the day came when I said we should leave. May 17, is a big holiday in Norway and our departure time. I decided that instead of waiting another day to leave, we would leave at noon and anchor in about three hours. It seems that leaving the dock is the hardest. Once under way it's easier to keep on schedule. At noon we had the boat filled, but still a lot of gear lay on the dock, with nowhere to put it. The temptation to wait another day was very strong, we could put things right and have another easy day ashore.

"Stuff everything below," I said, "we are leaving now." It was incredible we were actually leaving for Norway on my home-built boat!

For some reason, I don't remember why now, I didn't want to put the skiff on deck. Maybe I was planning to use it later, but Terry was to follow us out of the marina in the skiff, then we would tie it on behind. Anyway, we said our goodbyes to marina friends, backed out of the slip, and motored out to the bayou. Terry had trouble getting the outboard motor started and so started to row after us. Some of our friends came running along the shore trying to stop us, but we were already clearing the marina. Terry caught up to us and we took him aboard. There must have been a camera in the crowd because strange things seem to happen on boats when cameras are present.

We came to anchor in a small lagoon about three hours away from the marina. Now we had limited our choices of things to do. All we had was on the boat. We began sorting out our cargo and trying to make some sense of the main cabin. Did I say we had the motorcycle in the cabin too? It is dangerous to have things so out of place while at sea, for the basic fact, that one can't find anything in a hurry. Things need a home and to be put back when done using them. It was calm that night and later the fog rolled in.

By morning the fog was still with us. We decided to motor back to the entrance of the channel, and finish fueling up at a small fishing bait shop. We had saved this job for later, in that we had no way to haul fuel to the boat while we were at the marina. I had forgotten to do it while the motorcycle was still together. While we were at this bait shop, another boat came in. He was heading to Mobile,

Alabama for a boat show. "Where are you boys going," he asked? Norway! He was very interested in our names, a fact he thought would come in handy as he read some future news account of our failed trip, I thought. The fog lifted and we headed out for the last few miles till we hit the Mississippi Sound.

As we made our way to the last bridge, we called ahead for an opening. There would be a short wait, so we were going to circle. The current was moving out of the Rigolettes, so we kept circling with the motor on to keep some steerage. On one of our passes, Terry had gotten too close to the bridge and was turning with the current. I could see that we weren't going to make it without hitting the bridge. I shoved the throttle full forward to give the boat an extra boost to make it around. We cleared the pilings, but not by much. Not a fine way to start out. The bridge opened and we headed out.

We sailed through the day and it was dark before we came to anchor off Ship Island, about 10 miles south of Biloxi, Alabama. We would take a short break here and leave about mid-day tomorrow.

In the morning, Stuart and I took the skiff ashore to look around. I wanted Stuart to see the restored Civil War fort located there, Fort Massachusetts. We beached the skiff pulling it up far enough out of the water, so it wouldn't float away, we wouldn't be gone long anyway. We hadn't walked more than 10 or 15 minutes and Stuart had this uneasy feeling that he would like to go back to the skiff to check on things. I wanted to get across the island to see how the Gulf looked this morning, so I kept going, Stuart turned around. I walked for a while and got a good look at the south side of the island.

When I saw Stuart again he was soaking wet. "What happened," I asked him? He explained that when he got back to the skiff, the tide had taken it off the beach and he had to swim after it. This was not a good omen for the start of such a big trip. Stuart's appetite for more island exploring was over. He indicated he would like to return to the boat, maybe the anchor was dragging on that too. I took Stuart back and Terry was up now and we went ashore. Stuart remained on board keeping an eye on things.

By noon, we were ready to raise the anchor and sail around the west end of the island and shape a course for Ft. Myers, Florida. This time, I would try to make the coast of Florida early and work the land breezes down the coast. There is a predominant southeast wind coming up from Florida, and this is not good for a sailboat making for the southeast. We struck out across the gulf on a more easterly direction. We got a glimpse of Sarasota, Florida before turning south. The land breezes came in at night and we rode them south. We came into Ft. Meyers Beach and dropped the hook.

Terry and Stuart took the skiff ashore to check on bus schedules. Stuart planned to visit relatives on the east coast of Florida, before heading back to Minnesota. When they returned, they had learned that Stuart must strike out for Ft. Meyers right away, as the bus was leaving soon. There was not time to wait for a local bus either, so he hired a cab to take him into town. In a flash Stuart was gone. It's strange aboard a small sailboat when someone leaves. You spend so much time in close quarters with each other, that each person is a part of the whole. Then, when one leaves, there is this void that must be filled, an empty bunk, and an empty bench.

Now, Terry and I would ready the boat for the motor trip across the Okeechobee Waterway. This is a 200-mile canal and lake that cuts across the FL Peninsula, saving a few days travel around the tip of FL. The only drawback for us was this 50-foot railway bridge near the east side. We need exactly 48-feet 6-inches to clear. We also have a 2-foot antenna on top of that, but it can bend. We would take the gamble and motor across the peninsula, and in the end hope we could get through. If not, we would have a situation to think about.

We filled the fuel tanks, topped off the water and groceries, flushed the holding tanks in their pump-out on shore and motored out. The first night we anchored in La Belle. We met some nice folks there, and also got some laundry done before leaving. We passed through a couple of locks and the second night, we tied to some dolphin pilings. They are for commercial traffic and I suppose we shouldn't have been there, but they were empty and we couldn't find any other good place out of the way. We left early the next day. We passed an alligator and since it was the first one we had seen, I decided to go around for another look. We grounded on the mud bank. By wiggling the rudder back and forth and applying forward power we slid off. We entered Lake Okeechobee and the wind was in our favor. We had strayed a little out of the channel, and soon we felt the grating noise as the keel drug on a sandbar. The boat slowed, but before we came to a stop, the wind heeled us over to such an angle, that we slid off and began sailing again. We watched the channel markers more closely now.

We went through one more lock, and then reached the railway bridge. It looked very tight and as we approached,

Terry went to the bow to try judge things better. A few feet from the bridge, he yelled to slow down, I thought we were almost stopped anyway. As we coasted under the bridge, the 2-foot flexible antenna on top of the mast bent over halfway. It clicked across the beams till we reached the outside and snapped upright again. One more foot and we would have been stuck under the bridge. It was a relief to be on the east side of the bridge. Finally, we got lucky that time. I know we had been lucky too many times, soon it might run out.

When we neared Stuart, FL, we sailed past some houses with boat docks. There were some people on one of them and they yelled out to us to take them sailing. I wonder what they would have thought if they knew we were heading for Norway, still nine weeks of sailing away.

We found an anchorage and had trouble getting the anchor to stick. There was a current running, and it would be important to stay put or who knows where the boat would end up. We checked in with Bill on the ham radio, as to the whereabouts of the new crew, Ben and Roger. They would meet us in Shepard's Park, not very far from us, in the morning. They had flown down from Minneapolis to Orlando and rented a car. They were taking in some sights on the way down.

It was hot that night, and Terry slept on the deck. By morning his sleeping bag was wet with dew, but he enjoyed the fresh air. I took Terry ashore to look for the guys. I returned to the boat to straighten things up and make room for the two new crew members. They had found each other alright, and were waiting for me when I returned. We loaded their gear in the skiff and set off for *Indian Summer*. Roger had been aboard before, and knew the layout. We showed

Ben around and gave him a quick rundown on the gear.

The next day, we all went ashore and used the rental car for our big grocery run. Terry had made out a list and when we got to the supermarket, we all had certain items to get. We each took a cart and set off. We were provisioning for 50 days, however we could resupply in Bermuda, if we needed. Since we had no refrigeration we bought no packaged meat. The food in cans would have to be eaten the same day we opened them. When we got the carts out to the car, we quickly filled up the trunk. Terry and I got in the back seat and the rest of the groceries where piled on top of us. We drove back to the park and off loaded the groceries to the skiff, then ferried them out to the boat. I had taken the skiff with a full load of groceries out to the boat alone, as there was no room for the crew that trip.

When I got to the boat, I noticed that she had moved further out of the anchorage, the anchor was dragging. I unloaded the groceries and tied off the skiff. I pulled up the anchor and reset it. I made a fast trip back to shore to get the crew. I was anxious to get back aboard to make sure the anchor was holding. The shifting current must have twisted the anchor out. That evening, Terry took stock of what we had bought and decided that we needed to make another run to the store. Since a sailboat runs on food, not diesel, we wanted to make sure we had enough food. The next day, the crew went for more provisions.

We were still a few miles from the coast, and the outlet to the sea was questionable for our required depth. It looked safer to travel north along the Intracoastal Waterway, till we made the Ft. Pierce channel. Roger still had to drop off the rental car, the drop off point a bit north of the outlet. We would motor or sail to the channel, and wait for Roger to take the bus back to us. He would take a radio to reach us when he was ready to come off the shore.

We found an anchorage next to the outlet channel and set the hook. Terry dove on the anchor to check that it was dug in proper. He had to pull himself down along the anchor rode. It was dark down there, and he had to feel around to get an idea about the status of the anchor. It was hooked well. The current was strong and he needed to hang on tight to the rode as he came back up.

The next morning we went across the channel in the skiff to fill up our water and fuel jugs. We wanted everything to be topped-off before we set out. We would stop in Bermuda, 900 miles out. Roger called that afternoon. He had dropped of the rental car and was ready to be picked up. We spent a second night there, and set the following morning as departure day. In the morning, we got up early and got the skiff aboard. I had listened to channel 16 the day before, and noticed that they would give the channel conditions for the day. I still hadn't learned that traveling afloat was very different from traveling on land. Why would they give channel conditions? I would soon see why.

In my eager anticipation to get out to sea and begin the voyage, I had the crew pull-up anchor before all was stowed away. We still had three loose jugs of diesel fuel, the spare Danforth anchor, and an ice chest full of water in the cockpit. None of it tied down. These I thought could be dealt with while underway. As soon as the anchor broke free we were drifting with the strong current, so I put the transmission in gear and we started off. There were four of us, so I thought we could handle the multi tasks. The crew was mustered in the cockpit with no particular duty in mind. I didn't think of the potential disaster waiting us.

The current was flowing north, our direction of travel and with the engine cranking, we were going much too fast to make snap decisions. All of a sudden, the buoys in the channel didn't match the buoys on our new chart. By deduction, a bridge we just went under, we knew the channel was abeam. I made a quick right turn, cutting off a power boat coming into the intersection, a humbling start to such a major trip. Luckily for us, the power boater gave us room to maneuver. The fun was just starting.

As we moved out the channel, the waves turned very steep, abruptly the boat began hobby horsing and the extra gear started slamming back and forth in the cockpit. I had to give the boat full throttle just to keep her head straight out the channel, we were making very little progress and the rocks lining the sides of the channel didn't look very inviting either. Water was coming in large quantities, down the length of the deck as the bow would pick up a wave and throw it back. Then water would come in over the stern. I yelled to Ben and Roger to hang onto the gear while Terry tried to get it lashed in one spot. I quickly noticed a small group of fishermen standing on the rocks looking our way. I'll bet this channel provides a lot of entertainment on days like this. In a flash, I thought of the channel warning on the radio. Not all days are good days to go. When there is a wind blowing into the channel, it will bring with breaking steep seas. Funny how such basic things are overlooked, now I know for next time.

We cleared the channel without further incident and got into calmer waters. We raised the sails and shut the engine off. Our course was east by north, aiming for the northern tip of the Bahamas. I figured the Gulf Stream would carry us past the shallow banks of the Bahamas.

During the night, the traffic seemed to increase, with lots of ship traffic around. During the day, it is easy to recognize what is near and far. At night, lights show up both far and near away. One is not really sure if it is a small boat up close or a big ship far away. We had to keep a vigilant watch. On Roger's watch, he noticed a large grouping of lights cutting across our path, many lights on the same vessel, and then far behind, there was a small red light. We brought the binoculars into play and found that the boat with many lights, a tugboat, was pulling a huge vessel far behind. The towed vessel was sporting only a red light that we could see from our side. By deduction, we knew there had to be a cable between the two, and that we had better change our course to go around the towed vessel. Later that night, the wind died out and we drifted north with the current.

We had 900 miles to go to reach Bermuda, and the winds were becoming very stingy. When it blew it was from the east, and we were reluctant to get too far east, without getting some northing in. We could find ourselves way downwind of Bermuda, and not enough fuel to reach it. At times we ran the engine with the sails to climb up on the wind. With the engine and the main sail, we could motor sail much closer to the wind and nearer our destination. Finally, the wind became too light to do anything with it, so we stopped for a while.

The sun was bright and the water warm, so we took advantage of the situation and went swimming. Terry declined and would rather nap. After a refreshing swim, we started the engine and began the noisy trek to Bermuda, 125 miles away. We had enough fuel to reach it in the calm conditions, and we didn't have time to sit and wait for the right wind.

We approached Bermuda from the southwest and first saw Gibbs Hill Lighthouse. We gave the Bermuda radio a call on channel 16, and were advised to call when we got close to the cut into St. Georges. The tall ships race was about to begin and we would have a front row seat if we stayed out till they left. We approached the cut and stopped the engine. We had been motoring for two days and the silence was deafening. As we drifted and watched for the tall ships to appear, I noticed that the rudder was acting stiff when we moved the wheel from side to side. Terry volunteered to dive under the boat to check it out, maybe we had snagged something. He found nothing unusual and I made a note to grease the steering chain after we anchored in the bay.

Soon the tall ships came around the corner and with them scores of small boats. The area around us quickly filled with pleasure boats darting around, and in many cases the helmsman looking everywhere, but where his craft is going. We decide that it would be prudent to move and make our way to the anchorage. There were a few anxious moments with other boats before we got into the bay, but we got by them alright. We tied up at the customs house and presented our papers. We turned in our plastic flare gun for the duration of our stay, no guns of any sort allowed onboard.

While we waited for the paperwork to be completed, we met a local missionary, who keeps an eye out for new comers and invites them to his church. He gives them free access to the internet at the church, so we got the address to the church.

After the paperwork was completed, we motored out into the anchorage and set the hook down, 12 days from the time we left Florida. We would stay here until I received some boat documentation Marion had sent to us. I had left before renewing the boat papers, and even though everything was current now, by the time we reached our next landfall in the Shetlands, it would have run out. The crew immediately fanned out to explore the island.

There are many advantages to having crew, and one is the additional wealth of information each person picks up every day. It takes one man a lot of time to check out all the interesting things in a new place, but in our case it was divided by four.

Terry wanted to check into scuba diving. Roger was interested in taking the bus across the island. Ben wanted to learn more about Paul and the church he was working in. I just wanted to take a slow walk and take in all I could see at a relaxed pace. In the evening, we would all talk about our adventures. Terry had signed up for two dives. Roger was impressed by the bus trip, explaining how the roads were so narrow that many times branches would be striking the side of the bus, the trip to Hamilton, was worth it he exclaimed.

I had walked with Ben in that first afternoon, while he went looking for that church, Paul the missionary, had told us about. We were walking up this quiet street and saw a building that sure looked like the one we wanted. An older, black lady was raking her lawn next door so we inquired if we had found the right church. "Why yes honey, it is but they's all black," she said. We walked up to the church and found Paul and got service times for Sunday. I joined Ben when he went to church and we felt welcome enough even though we were the only white guys there.

We spent some of the time overhauling the boat interior. We had kept some items that we couldn't bear to toss when we left Slidell, and now that we had experience with walking and working around them, we knew it would be better to give them away or toss them in the trash. We needed open space. We did try to give the stuff away and what we couldn't give away, we threw.

I had noticed that the topside paint was coming off in sheets, and apparently the paint had not stuck very well, this was disappointing. I tried to paint over the bare spots, but being so close to the waterline, it didn't work very well. Bare steel rusts very fast in salt water, and though the strength is still there, the boat hull looked terrible. By the time we got to Norway, all the paint around the waterline was gone and one fellow boater thought we had been sailing in some ice that had scraped the paint off.

Roger had allowed some time to see the island and now was preparing to leave for home via the airport. He had gone below to pack. Roger just hates to carry luggage when he travels, and so his tactic is to wear everything that he couldn't give away to his fellow crew mates. When Roger announced that he was ready to be hauled ashore, he was a plump sight, besides wearing his extra clothes, he had on a ski vest. Terry commented that he may have trouble at the airport. We ferried Roger ashore to the bus stop and he was gone. He had been a good addition to the crew and his infectious humor would be missed. His bunk on the port side of the engine now lay empty. It would take some time to get used to his absence.

My documentation had not arrived yet and I was getting anxious to assign a departure date. We had 3,100 miles to go. Terry and I overheard some American sailors talking about the trip over from the states; straight across from the states their track had covered about 700 miles. Somehow that didn't seem like such a big trip to us now.

Terry's scuba dives had been postponed due to rain. It would be pretty nasty to be caught out in the rain while preparing to dive to 30-feet of water, so it was set for a sunnier day. This was a little hard to understand, but my papers hadn't come yet anyway.

The long awaited letter came and I set June 20 as departure day. We still had bus tickets left, so on the 19th we took a trip to the other side of the island and rode the ferry across the bay. It was a full day, and on the bus ride back to the boat, I requested that it would be a good idea for all of us to get to bed early. Terry had just bought an underwater light and had planned to go night diving before we left. This was not in the best interest of the impending voyage and I tried to persuade him to get a good night sleep before we left, but he was determined to go. Well, since I had neglected to build in a brig in the boat, I couldn't make him stay. He was on his own getting back to the boat, we would not wait up for him, to ferry him back to the boat.

Ben and I went out to the boat and took our bunks early. Sometime in the early hours of the morning, I heard the deep sea diver climb aboard, we were a team again.

There are so many dangers lurking around just waiting to derail the trip, I just hated to take many extra chances. I have been crew before, and it is very different than skipper. A lot of responsibility to see through a safe and successful adventure falls to the skipper as it should. The crew may feel a little of this, but in the end, if it doesn't work out, they don't have as much invested.

I arose early to get a good jump on the day, and also because I couldn't wait any longer to get started. The big adventure would begin today. Once we left Bermuda, it would be difficult, if not impossible, to turn around. We would try to get *Indian Summer* into the east bound Gulf Stream and westerly winds, all would be in our favor for once. The day before, some Norwegians we had met in Bermuda, had left. They were on a 33-foot boat name *Sinora Sling,* and now we would be trailing in their wake. We had hoped to sight them, and be able to talk to them by radio, but we would need to be 20 miles or closer to do this. There was another Norwegian boat called *Second,* that would leave in a few days. He was familiar with the coastline where we would make our landfall, and showed us a short cut through the rocks into the fjords. We had said our goodbyes and given them our leftover bus tickets we hadn't used.

I gave Marion a call before we left; I had been calling most days. I was looking for a reassuring word from her that we would do just fine. The call turning into a biting lecture from her and I felt much worse when I hung up. I guess she had a few things to get off her chest and what better time than now. I felt even worse when I found out my phone bill was 500 dollars that month. I felt my calls didn't help either of us much.

With our water tanks and every container that could hold drinking water filled, we pulled our anchor, next stop

Lerwick, Shetland Islands, 3,100 miles away. We were gambling everything, that we could meet every challenge in the next six weeks. We would have to sail or motor north, till we found the Gulf Stream and westerly winds. We were still too far south to head east. During the summer, there is a large high pressure system, that lays between Bermuda and the Azores, this we would have to avoid, as there is no wind in that area. The wind was light as we rounded the island and started north. We would keep the motor on till we were far enough away from the island.

When starting a voyage this long, it is important to get away from land as soon as possible, should bad weather develop, we would need sea room to wait it out. We have a few tactics in our bag to deal with deteriorating weather; storm sails, storm anchor, laying a hull and running before the advancing waves. The main idea is to hold the current position, so running before the storm would be the last resort. It may take days to regain our position again. For five days we maintain a northerly course, the wind being very light. When we reached latitude 39 degrees, about even with New York City, we began picking up westerly winds and we could see the effects of the Gulf Stream on our course, as we were pulled east, when our heading was due north. We began our easterly sail and as the days rolled by, we were experiencing more wind from aft of the starb'd quarter. Very seldom did the wind get over 20 knots, but mostly stayed in the 12 to 15 knot range. We got daily runs of 105 to 120 miles noon to noon.

We were sailing in the Gulf Stream and feeling the effects of the current added to our speed. Not a huge amount, but every little bit helped. One day our noon to noon mileage was 140 miles due to a steady wind. Of course, this kind of wind increases the wave action, so the extra 30 miles were paid for with increased discomfort. Now, I know 30 miles seems like a small distance, but divide this by six knots, our speed, and you get five more hours of rocking and rolling added to the previous 19, it makes a difference.

This was easy sailing. With the wind vane steering the boat, all the watch had to do was monitor our course, keep an eye on chaffing lines and watch out for shipping. With three as crew, we had watches of two hours on and four hours off. When it came to sail changes, at least one member would help, but mostly we all three would do it, if we were all awake. The temperature was nice, swimming trunks and tee shirts, anything else was too hot.

As we neared the Azores, actually about 500 miles away, we could see that the Gulf Stream had separated and the half we were on was pulling us southerly, even though our heading was due east. We tacked the boat and sailed north to reach the north bound current.

We were making such good time, that on one of my ham radio calls to Bill Landby, I had him tell Marion a date we would be in Lerwick. I never should have done that, because as we were coming to the top of Scotland a strong northeast wind blew up and stopped us dead in our tracks. We tried to sail against it by tacking back and forth and after two days of sailing, for 24 hours each day, we had only advanced three miles toward Lerwick. The wind was so strong, that we kept being blown sideways, as we sailed forward. On the third day, we just waited it out and let the wind blow us backwards. After that strong blow, came a dead calm, we still couldn't sail. We did have enough fuel to get us closer to Lerwick, so we started motoring. Towards the end we did get a fair wind again, and sailed into Lerwick in style.

About 10 miles or so from the town, we noticed a Coast Guard helicopter circling around a power boat, and then on the VHF radio, we heard the helicopter crew ask the power boat if they would help them in a practice rescue. A lady on the boat answered back, in broken English, after a couple of requests that she didn't know what they wanted. I don't think they wanted her to jump in the water, but maybe they would have one of the helicopter crew board their boat and practice jumping out of it to be hoisted up. Well, after it was clear she was totally confused, they just told her to disregard everything they said and have a nice day. Since water is such a part of their lives on the island, because many people work on the water, it's kind of like a volunteer fire department. It's quite an honor for residents to serve and it can be very risky business too.

We called the harbor master at Lerwick to say we were an American boat docking at the small boat harbor and would need customs. He told us since it was Sunday, nobody was on duty so just go in, tie up and he would send someone over on Monday. He also said we were free to go uptown to buy anything we needed. I took an immediate liking to Shetlands on hearing this.

When we motored up to the dock, there was a couple waiting there to take our lines. They said that when they heard there was an America boat coming in, they wanted to come down to greet us. How is that for a welcoming?

We had arrived five days later than I had told Marion

and her flight over had been delayed so she missed the weekly ferry too. She just went to her relatives to visit till the next ferry, a week later, would go. The islands are about 200 miles from Norway.

My ham radio calls had been getting later as we moved east, due to atmospheric conditions and now it was midnight before I could reach Bill to tell him we had arrived. We were all so tired from the excitement of making landfall that we had not slept. So Terry went to bed and Ben kind of dozed on the couch, while I sat on the top steps leading into the cabin, waiting for midnight to make the call. The top step is about four feet up from the cabin floor. As I sat there so tired I finally fell asleep. When I dozed off, I fell forward from the steps. As I did, I woke up and tried to run to get my legs under me. Well, I did, but when I hit the floor, I was running and ran fast forward just missing the five-inch by six-foot steel compression post located in the middle of the cabin. I'm sure my injuries would have been serious if I would have struck the post at full speed, I was very lucky. I did wake up Ben as I ran past him, scaring the daylights out of him too. I did make the call to Bill and everyone was relieved that the big trip was behind us. Only 200 miles to Norway, first we will wait for the ferry to bring Marion to us. She had decided to sail the last and maybe most dangerous part of the trip with us. There are many off lying rocks on Norway's shore and it was going to be tricky getting through them.

The custom agent that checked us in was Robbie L. and we became good friends with him and his wife Norra. We met Marion as planned when the ferry arrived a few days later. We bought a few more groceries and saw some sights around the island. We heard there was a sailboat race to a neighboring island and we were invited to participate. *Indian Summer,* was not a race boat, but they said we should come anyway, as there would be an annual dance when a lot of people come besides the racers. It was on our way to Norway so we said we would go.

On the morning we were to leave, there were still a few bags of recycle items like cans and bottles. I had gotten a little tired of these bags in our limited space on the boat and was anxious to have Terry get rid of them. He was in charge of the recycle stuff. They were still lying in the cockpit just before leaving, and Terry said they didn't recycle here and he couldn't just dump them in the trash like the islanders do. He had a last minute errand to do. While he was gone, I elected to dump the trash myself. After two months at sea, I think we both had a short fuse. When Terry came back I cast off and while motoring away, he inquired to his recycle bags. I told the truth, they decided to stay in Lerwick. At this, he decided to throw some eggs over that were from caged chickens. It was getting silly, and I decided that if that would make him happy I would just let it go. Six dollars' worth of eggs was a good trade for finally getting rid of the recycle bags. Terry decided to mutiny and for the next few hours decided not to be a part of the crew.

Well, we made it alright, to the Out Skerries and rafted up to a group of boats. It was an exciting time that evening, we got to watch some good local dancing and meet a few more people. When we started to tell people where we had come from, they would stop us and say they have already heard about it. In a small community, news travels fast. We met Robbie and Norra there too. They had raced over in a sailboat.

The next day, it was blowing fearful from the west and I felt sorry for the sailboats sailing back to Lerwick against it. We decided to hang out for another day and explore the island. There are three that are called Out Skerries and about 80 people live on them. They have two stores that open at different times to accommodate each other. They sell groceries and hardware, everything you would need to live, maybe not much extra though.

The following day, it was still blowing hard, but since it was from the west and we were going east, it would be good sailing for us. We left the harbor and just put up the smaller staysail. We got right up to hull speed, that's the fastest a displacement hull can go, and hung on. Of course, we all got sick, but we were really moving and we hand steered all the way across, 175 miles from the islands. I was worried about the coast of Norway in such a wind, but as we closed in on the coast, the wind let up and we had no trouble coming in through the rocks. With the waves spraying high above them as they crashed into the rocks, they weren't hard to see.

It was late in the afternoon when we came through the rocks on the coast, and Bergen was still about 20-miles inland, so I wanted to tie up for the night. At first I tried anchoring, but it was too deep and figured it would be just rock on the bottom anyway, nothing for the anchor to dig into. I noticed a small cove off to one side with an empty dock and warehouse next to it. I motored over to it and tied up. No one was around to ask about staying there, so we all decided to go for a walk and find the owner.

A short hike up the hill and we found a road and there met a fellow who directed us to the owner's house. He said we walk down the road and when we come to, he hesitated, some "special birds," turn left to his house. We left and continued down the road wondering what special birds could be. We came to a pen with peacocks in, the special birds, turned left and found the owner's house. He was home and graciously let us stay tied there for the night. It would be the theme all through Norway, people helping us when asked.

The next day, we cast off and sailed through the fjords to Bergen. We were not used to boats rafting up, but it is common all through Norway, where one boat is tied to shore and as many as four boats tied to him. This we saw, was the way to tie up in Bergen, so we picked a likely boat and nuzzled up to him.

Ben stayed with us for a few days till some of his friends came to pick him up. I got the passports stamped and also got permission to leave the boat in Norway through the following year, without paying an import tax. *The Bergen Tieden* paper, a main paper in Bergen, sent a reporter down to interview us, and got written up on the back page the next day. I still don't know why they chose us, since most Norwegian boats are like fine pieces of furniture and we were a rusty hulk. Maybe they were surprised we could come so far in a homemade steel boat. I was proud of her though.

In a few days, we left Bergen to sail to the Hardanger Fjord and Norheimsund, where Marion has relatives. We did stop in Uskadalen after leaving Bergen, as it is about the halfway mark to Norheimsund. There we met a few more Norwegians sailors. Three of them were readying their boat to go around the world, and then there was Knute who invited us over for waffles.

When we came into Norheimsund, Marion's relatives were waiting for us on the dock. They had one relative who lived a ways up the fjord and he was watching, with binoculars, for us who sounded the alarm to the others when we were spotted. Among the group was Gundrun, she was in her 80's, and was waving the Norwegian flag and we sure felt welcome. The hospitality never ceased all the time we were there.

There was much to do, but first coffee and cakes. Later Terry and I took the motorcycle out of the boat, it was in pieces, and assembled it. Then we pushed it over to one of the relative's barn. We would try using it in Norway next year. I also had a major paint failure, on the top-side paint and also the deck. I just slapped on some paint to cover the surface rust, till I could get it sandblasted or ground later.

We had such a good time visiting and hated to leave, but it had taken all summer to cross the ocean and now we had to go home.

2001 Vacation Boot Camp, Cruising
the Coast of Norway

This was one jam-packed summer and even now found it hard to believe we did all those things.

June 3, was Erin's high school graduation party at our home. She would come with us to Norway and visit relatives, then fly home when Marion and I would start sailing. The next day we had loaded up the van and were driving to Minneapolis. Before we got very far, I noticed a vibration in the front end, so decided to turn around and take it back to my shop to see what the problem was. I thought it might be just an out of balance tire. When I got a chance to study it, it was a bad axle that was the problem. I got the parts store manager, Mark, to open up the store for me; it was a weekend, so I could buy the axle. I took it home and replaced it. Unfortunately, I changed the wrong one, so back again to get the opposite axle and soon I had it fixed and we were on the way. We stopped a few places on the way to Minneapolis to visit friends and relatives. It's a 365-mile trip to the airport, so we like to stop for a break.

On June 6, we flew out of Minneapolis for Reykjavik, then to Oslo and on to Bergen. The three of us had a combined luggage of six bags and I was happy to see that Mikjell had brought a station wagon to pick us up in. We really don't bring so many clothes. Actually, hardly any as we leave clothes on the boat for next year, but we had a lot of boat parts and even a motorcycle tire.

The next few weeks were spent between visiting, eating, and working on the boat. Marion's brother, Paul from Chicago and a daughter, Jennifer from Milwaukee, came to Norway also. We were shown all around, even taken up into the mountains to see where they used to keep cattle in the summer time, a long time ago. Mikjell and Kristi were building a cabin at another place in the mountains, so we got a good tour of that also. Mikjell had planted trees as a young boy at this spot, and now they were large enough to build a cabin with some of them. We had such a good time with the relatives. They made our stay there so memorable. We will never forget their kindness.

One of the interesting happenings took place while we were still in Norheimsund was during the month of June.

During midsummer, the town hosts a wooden boat festival. A lot of classic boats come to exhibit, plus there are vendors and demonstrators at the wooden rebuild shop, located in the town. Here they show how early boat builders did their work. They also invite some speaker to give a talk and this year they asked me. I was humbled by the thought of talking to a group of sailors who really know something of boats. My *Indian Summer,* being built of steel, was a far cry from the boats in Norway, but they told me that we both had to work with the oceans ways, wood or steel. I agreed to do it, thinking that maybe not many would understand English anyway. In this I was mistaken, finding out that English was their second language. I survived the talk and I don't think anyone left early or fell out of their chairs from boredom. I tried to keep it short with just a few slides to show.

It always seems to take a couple of weeks before we are ready to go, and this time I had more projects to do, as I was close to a lumber yard, I would redo the forward bunk. When I first built it, I hadn't allowed enough head room, after the thick foam for a cushion was in place. Our noses were too close to the ceiling. Now I had a chance to get some plywood to redo it, by dropping it down.

On June 25, Marion and Gerd, another relative of Marion's, took Erin to the airport in Bergen, so she could fly home.

June 27, we sailed away from Norheimsund, to travel back to Bergen and points north. We stopped in Uskadalen again, before coming to Bergen. After a few days in Bergen, we had seen most everything we wanted to, it was time to go. We sailed north trying to stay close to the open ocean. We found many islands with small communities on them and people were so friendly. When we got to Norfjord, we traveled up the fjord to Nordfjordeid, where we located a small dock in the town.

I had loaded the motorcycle, 400 Kawasaki, on the deck and tied it to the mast. Since we weren't going to be in heavy water, I was sure it would be alright. I did cover it with a tarp, partly to protect it from the weather, and also I didn't want to explain to everyone we met, what it was doing on the boat. At this dock, we unloaded the motorcycle and planned to do a little inland exploring with it. First, we called up some relatives of neighbors back home and were soon invited to supper one night. We came on the Kawasaki.

The next few days were spent traveling on the bike and staying at hostels. We rode down into the Geiranger Fjord and took the ferry across and back on the motorcycle, eventually coming back to the boat. When we were about to load the bike back on the boat, the folks who we had visited with, came by at just the right time and gave us a hand wheeling it on deck. As a precaution, I attached a halyard line from the mast to the bike and Marion would keep a tight line on it as I wheeled it aboard. I sure didn't want it to topple over the side while on the narrow plank.

We sailed back south again stopping at interesting islands, one called in English, The Norwegian Horse, and we climbed to the top. Norway has a neat custom of letting people experience the mountains, so land owners let hikers cross their property if possible. This was the case here, and when we arrived, the owner knew what we wanted even though he couldn't speak English. He had marked a path up the side of the mountain, but it was steep in places. When I got to the top, I radioed down to Marion what a great view it was, since it was on the edge of the mainland. Marion said she would try coming up too. While I waited for her, I saw a glass jar with a note pad and pencil inside, stuffed in a niche in a rock cairn. It was for people that climbed the mountain to sign their names and boat name, which I did. Marion hadn't come yet, so I started back down. She had come about halfway and had had enough of mountain climbing already. She did get a good view of the surroundings from there too, so we headed back to the boat.

When we reached the Sogne Fjord, we parked the boat again at a small village and unloaded the bike. We did some trips around there, and found another mountain to climb. This one, by perseverance, Marion made it to the top. What a great view it was! There were cairns built of rocks, like the last one. Later, we rode to the east end of the fjord and ferried across. Then on to Norheimsund, getting lost on the way and ending up in someone's yard. In Norheimsund, we stored the bike in Gerd and Mikal's barn again, and took a series of buses back to the boat.

Next, we sailed back down to Bergen, where we would meet up with Joe McDonnell's son, Joey. He was on a summer tour of Europe and had just arrived from the states. He had expressed an interest in sailing with us, and it was agreed that he should meet us in Bergen, and help us sail out to the Shetlands to park the boat. I had to leave Norway with the boat, as I was only allowed so much time to keep it there without paying an import tax. We met Joey at the train station and boarded the boat. While we motored the 20 miles out to the ocean from Bergen, Marion had fixed a nice lunch for us to eat before getting out on the ocean.

However, when we saw the sea conditions we were

going to sail in, I knew we were all going to be sick for a while. It was too much too soon. The wind was strong from the north, and that was a good direction for us, but it would be rough going by the looks of the waves, lots of white horses out there. We tightened down everything and reefed in the sails before leaving the protection of the small bay we were in. As soon as we cleared the protection of the channel we were in, the wind grabbed onto the sails, we heeled over and started moving--fast. It was exhilarating sailing and of course the nice lunch came up--fast too.

While we were still in range of Bergen weather reports, Marion heard on the VHF radio, "Attention all ships, attention all ships turn to station twenty-something." When we did, we heard the weather forecast in Norwegian. It was helpful for those that speak the language, but not for us. Well, I told Marion no matter what they said we weren't turning back; we're too far out now. I had checked with the weather station by phone while in Bergen harbor before we left, and they read off the forecast to me in English. I hadn't heard anything bad coming that we couldn't handle.

Another event that happened was a little wrestling match with me and the jib sail, up on the fore deck on our way across the North Sea. It had been tied to the forward railing since we were only using the smaller stays'l and a boarding sea had washed it over the side. It was all I could do to get it back aboard while Joey kept us on course. He didn't dare leave the wheel to help me. When I checked in on Marion she was sitting on the floor, with most everything that had been on the shelves lying around her, some broken glass too, but at least she couldn't fall or get thrown any farther down than the floor. I didn't say anything as she just sat there looking dazed.

We reached Lerwick harbor in two days, two very rough days from Bergen. The slip where I was to winter the boat was on the other side of the island in Scalloway. Six miles across from Lerwick, but 40 miles by boat as we had to sail down to the tip, 20 miles, then back 20 miles. It was foggy when we left Lerwick, so we used the GPS and radar to get us there. We couldn't see any of the islands, trusting to the electronics, is not always a good thing.

When we came to the entrance to the harbor on the other side of the island, we of course couldn't see it, and I hated to wait out in the fog, lest I get hit by another boat. We motored slowly in and the first thing we heard was the sound of large waves crashing on the rocks. Then came the opening in the rocks into the harbor, we were exactly where we should be. It was a relief to be safely in, after sailing that close to land and not even having a glimpse of it. We tied up the boat and caught the bus back to Lerwick, just in time to catch the weekly ferry back to Bergen. Joey had left from Lerwick for Aberdeen, Scotland to continue his tour.

As if we hadn't had enough travel yet, we took the bus partway to Oslo, and stopped at Honefoss to visit my relatives. We had seen them back in 1972, and it was so nice to get acquainted again. Later by bus, on to Oslo and home. It was a full summer with many schedules to meet and that can be a problem with a sailboat. Somehow we managed it.

2002 Shetland to Portugal

This year Marion and I would fly back to Norway, visit with her relatives in Norheimsund for a while, then take our motorcycle out of their barn, ride it to Bergen, where we would board the weekly ferry to Lerwick, Shetland Islands, and reunite with our boat stored in Scalloway, on the west side of the main island. Then, after riding around the island for a week or so, load it all up and sail down to Portugal. We had three months to do this, before Marion had to be back teaching in school, and I should be back in my welding shop, trying to earn a living again. It was an ambitious plan.

On June 4, we left Wannaska for Thief River Falls and had breakfast with our youngest daughter Erin. Then drove over to John and Sara's, our oldest daughter, to finish up paperwork from my work, and also finish packing. Clothes are not as important as hardware and spare parts that would be hard to find once we were underway. We made a stop in St. Cloud to visit our other boating friends, Clink and Ret Wilson. Clink was still working on his boat, and we spent a lot of time talking sailing and building. We spent the night there, and the next day our middle daughter Mary, drove up from Minneapolis to get us and she will join us, going to Norway, to meet the relatives.

June 6, Mary's friend, Jill took us to the airport and we flew out to Oslo. Mary has a previous friend, MayBritt, who lives close to Oslo, so we spent two days in Oslo, so Mary could visit her and so we could see some sights around town. Saturday, June 8, we arrived in Norheimsund and stayed at Kirsti and Mikjell Valland's home. We were again treated to a grand welcome and were taken around many places. I even found time to ready the boat for the coming sailing season.

Mary flew home on June 17, and the next day I rode the motorcycle to Bergen, 60 miles away, while Marion took the bus and five bags of luggage on the bus to Bergen. I met her at the bus stop in Bergen, and we got a taxi to take her and the bags of luggage to the ferry. I rode the bike over to the ferry and got a ticket to board. A few other bikes were coming too, and as it turned out, there was an annual biker rally happening in the Shetlands while we would be there.

Eleven and one half hours later, we arrived in Lerwick, Shetland. Marion met a fellow who works for the ferry line, while on the ferry, and he offered to haul our luggage to the hostel. I would ride the bike over. The boat would be too full of sailing gear to find a spot to lie down, so we spent the first night in the hostel. It's the best hostel we've seen and reasonably priced. We were glad to find this out.

June 21, we arrived at the boat and got it cleared out, so we could sleep there that night. One of the halyards had chaffed through, and I had to go to the top of the mast, to run a messenger down to pull up the halyard. Marion used the halyard winch to haul me up 50-feet to the top, this procedure she is not too happy about, but she is the only one around to do it.

It's so nice to have the motorcycle here to go places. We spent time riding the motorcycle around the island, attending musical programs we found out about, and working on the boat.

The boat had collected a lot of growth while spending the nine months in the slip, and needed to be cleaned off.

There were also many jelly-fish swimming in the water around the boat, and I was a little worried about them; however a local fisherman said they wouldn't harm me. I took a chance and drove in to clean the rudder and propeller. I came out without any problems from them.

Finally, July 6, we got underway, sailing to Fair Isle first, about 25-miles away. There was a music festival advertised there, and we sailed in tandem with another sailboat. The owner, Dominic, a young lady wanted to sail her boat there also, but hadn't sailed too far with her boat yet, and was happy to have someone to sail with. We agreed to take pictures of each other's boats, and exchange the roll of film once we got there. It has been difficult to get good pictures of my boat while sailing, it's just not safe to set someone off in a skiff, while there are good sailing conditions.

The festival was fun to go to and many people came by way of the ferry that travels between Lerwick and Fair Isle. I think there are only 60 year-round residents that live on the island normally, but there appeared to be many more at the program that night. We only stayed that day. There was a BBQ the next day on the beach, and we were invited, but the navtex weather monitor indicated bad weather coming in two days. It would be smart to leave the next day.

We left for Westray, in the Orkney Islands and arrived in the harbor about 10:00 p.m. We rafted up to the ferry for the night, because we didn't know where else to tie up to, it being too dark. Our boat was acting so strange, not wanting to sail very well, so the next day we motored over to the sea wall, at high tide, and tied her off to the mooring bits on the quay. At low tide, we saw huge clumps of seaweed stuck to the bottom. No wonder we had a hard time sailing, by dragging all that seaweed through the water.

While in Westray, Marion had had enough fun and told me she would probably fly home from Dublin. I had arranged to meet Ben and Alex in Dublin, for the sail to Portugal anyway, and she thought we could manage just fine without her. I wasn't really sure the boys were coming, so it meant I would sail to Portugal alone. I was hoping she would change her mind, but anything could happen between now and then, and not all of them good. I don't think she realizes how much I depend on everyone to help when we leave the dock. If someone leaves, there is an empty spot to fill, and not very easily done with limited crew.

July 13, 4:00 a.m., I got up to see daylight out and I wanted to get going. We had the west bound tide to catch. We rounded the northeast corner of the island and headed for Cape Wrath. By evening, we were north and 10-miles away from the Cape. I stopped sailing and we waited for daylight. I had to get up many times at night watching for traffic; it was bumpy with the wind blowing 18 knots. We were in a spot were most traffic would travel too. By 4:00 a.m. it was light enough to go sailing again. I had to keep tacking back and forth, trying to make progress to a place called Badcall Bay, but we were making very little progress. Suddenly, a great blast of wind came shrieking across the water and slammed into us. That told me it was time to get the engine running, and we were quickly hauling straight for the bay to get out of the fierce wind.

Other than an anchorage, we didn't find much there. We went ashore looking for a restaurant that was listed in our books, but it was only for reservations, we couldn't even buy coffee. This area is very remote and we shouldn't have expected too much. Later we worked our way down to Kyle of Lochalsh, and tied up to a pontoon. While there another steel boat came in, a 34-foot Bruce Roberts design, constructed of steel. It was for sale. We had a good visit with the couple sailing her. Their names were Roger and Pamela, and later we found out that our friend Robbie and his wife Norra, had bought this boat. Roger had mentioned to Robbie, that he had seen another steel Bruce Roberts boat, in Scotland, and of course Robbie knew of us from our stop in the Shetlands. It's a small world at times.

While in Kyle of Lochalsh, we took the bus to visit Eilean Donan, a restored castle. We could only spend about one hour there, due to the bus schedule. The castle looked just like we would have imagined a castle to be. They did have some demonstrators there, showing how things were done back in those days. This castle started out in the 13th century, was destroyed in 1719, and rebuilt in the early 20th century.

After Kyle of Lochalsh, we sailed to Inverie. There are no roads to this place, hiking or by boating are the only ways to get there. We went ashore to the Old Forge Pub and had some nice visits with locals. At midnight, the generator was shut off and candles were lit. I asked just what they do here, and it sounds like they are an outfitter for hunters and hikers. They called hunting, stalking. A while back, there was a music jam held at the pub, and we were given a free recording of the event. When we had come ashore in the skiff, we had pulled it high up on the beach and after midnight the tide had receded a lot, and now our little boat was far from the water's edge. I had to wonder just what

Marion was thinking when she climbed into the boat, before we had brought it to the water. We both had a good laugh over that.

Next stop Tobermory. Marion was determined to go to Edinburgh, so we took the bus from Tobermory, the ferry to Oban, then the train to Edinburgh. We found a music and dance program to go to, and a hostel to stay in. It was memorable for its condition. The worst in our travels, but we had a place to sleep, and the breakfast was augmented with food we carried along. After walking around town for a while, we returned the same way we came; train, ferry and bus. I think for me, the most I got out of the trip, was the different modes of travel it took to get there. I hope Marion found some fun in it and would be willing to stay with the boat to the end of summer. We spent a little time in Tobermory, and I remember how colorful the buildings were downtown. A brochure we read about the town, tells about the colorful buildings downtown and how they remind one of cities in the Mediterranean. One night, while anchored there, we were awakened by lights and voices right outside our boat. It turned out some sailor had fallen overboard and people were searching for him. I think he was later found onshore alive and well.

July 23, and we're set to go again. Riding the current down the west side of Scotland was exciting. We seemed to be flying. Passing Oban, we traveled through some over-falls due to the changing direction of the current. It would be deadly in a small fishing boat to be caught in them. We bounced and plunged through them. When the current direction changes, we had to look for a place to anchor for the night, out of the foul current. We gingerly motored closer to shore and dropped the hook; it stuck and we hoped it stayed that way the rest of the night. This evening, Marion says, if things don't start to get more "fun" she's leaving. I hated to tell her this is as "fun" as it could get.

I got up at 1:45 a.m. to check on the anchor, we were very close to a pile of rocks and with the wicked current we moved around a lot. By checking the tide chart, I see we couldn't leave till 7:00 a.m., to ride the south bound current. Pulling up anchor, we got into the stream again, heading for Gigha Sound. Holy cow we were moving, nine knots on the GPS, almost three times faster than we were used to. The current had got us and was sweeping us south. When the current has you in its grips, it's important to run the engine fast also, to keep water moving past the rudder. It's the only way we can steer. We were warned to stay away from a certain island, because of a whirlpool that forms when the current runs strongest. I was sure to avoid that area.

Coming into Gigha Island to anchor, the engine exhaust is giving off a lot of steam and not much water. The impeller that pumps cooling water to the engine had failed. I had to shut down the engine and we drifted, while I looked for a used spare one to install. Marion kept an eye out so we didn't drift into trouble, while I worked on the engine. Afterwards, we came to anchor and took the skiff ashore. I promised Marion a restaurant meal. While at the restaurant we meet a couple on another boat and they invited us over for a visit. They had seen us come in and knew we were strangers. Their boat was nice, 43-feet, and custom built. He was a boat surveyor and of course would have a nice boat. Later in Portugal, we met others sailors who have used him to survey their boat.

Leaving Gigha, we tack back and forth on our way south. While we were sailing close to the headland, Mull of Kintyre, a huge wave pops up, due to the backwash of waves hitting the cliff and coming back out. Marion was steering, and doesn't realize that wave could very easily break over us. She thinks it's fun, but I don't and quickly start the engine to drive out of there fast. We got a fast ride around the headland and were soon in the Irish Sea. The current did let up and we coasted along in a calm sea. We made for the closest point of land where we could anchor, Carnlough, Ireland. We didn't enter the breakwater in the harbor, but found good anchorage right outside.

The next day, we continued south and anchored off Ballycarry. This place has an enclosed harbor with breakwaters, and it was tempting to enter its high tide. As we motor in, Marion was checking the depth and couldn't find anything deep enough to float us at low water, so we went outside and anchored behind some rocks for protection from the wind. Six hours later, the harbor had dried out totally, and we are so glad we didn't stay in there.

Next was Bangor, just outside Belfast. We found a marina to tie to and went uptown for a walk-around. We asked at the marina if we could use their computer to check e-mail, but they couldn't let us use it.

Then, Ardglass, was the next port. We had a fair wind south and while sailing nicely, I spotted with binoculars, someone waving at us quite a distance away, but upwind. Oh how I hated to go back upwind, but we are about 10 miles off the coast of Ireland and if he needed assistance I needed to help. So back around we went, plowing into the wind. It took some time to get there and what we found was scuba divers putting on their wet suits, they were not signaling to us. I felt foolish, but as we rounded them we just waved and raised sail again. We still made Ardglass in daylight, but it was raining and we were soaked. Marion didn't want to stay below, so she sat next to me and I don't believe much was said. The marina really dried out at low tide, but they had good buoys marking the way in, with some cardinal markers showing a very bad area to stay away from. As the harbor master took our lines, Marion said, "I'm sure glad to be here." He looked at her dripping wet and says, "I bet you are too."

We still had a few days to get to Dublin, when Ben and Alex would arrive, so we could take our time here. We spent the day looking for a place to e-mail and ended up in a fellow's bedroom using his computer. The community center, where there were computers to use, was closed for the day. This total stranger even brought us tea and muffins while we checked on messages from home. He commented as we said our goodbyes, that he believed what the Bible says about entertaining strangers, because they could be angels. We assured him we definitely were not angels, but thanked him for his kindness to strangers.

The next day, our departure day, was totally fogged in, we stayed put all day. We did go to a fancy golf course that was supposed to have the best meals in town. We found it to be an excellent meal. Time was running out for us, now the boys would be in Dublin in two days, and we were still 60 miles away.

July 30, when we got going, the wind was perfect and westerly on the starb'd beam, our fastest point of sail; we seemed to fly towards Dublin and later the wind veered to the north still good for us. By 6:30 p.m. we were tied up at

Howth near Dublin. The boys came at 10:30 the next morning, so for a sailboat connection that's cutting it very close. We were happy to see them. Ben Nelson we knew from the trip across the ocean in 2000 and Alex Yamrik was a friend of Ben's.

In Howth, I found a marina store to get a few impellers for the engine. The used one I had used to replace the bad one in Gigha, had failed and I was using another worn-out one. We spent five days in Dublin, checking out the town and going out to Powers Court, a place Marion wanted to see, and we saw a show called Ragus that we liked. After the show, it was late and we were running to get to the station, not really knowing the shortest route. We saw a policeman and quickly asked him the fastest way to get to the station, his response, "by helicopter." Big help. Well, we missed the Dart transit out to Howth, but found a bus going that way later.

August 4, departure day at 8:00 a.m. and fogged in. We couldn't go, so I told the boys to meet back at the boat at 12:00 noon and we'll see what conditions are like. While we were waiting for the fog to lift, the marina came out to say my credit card, that I paid the slip rent with, was denied. I had another card that they tried and that was OK. Now, I wondered why my card wasn't OK, so I had to first find a store to buy a phone card. Then, call the card company back in the states. They were concerned about the locations that the card was being used in, sort of odd traveling places we had used it in, so to be safe they put a stop to it. Once they knew we were traveling through different countries by sailboat, the red flag was lifted. By now it was about time for the boys to return, the fog was gone. At 12:00 noon we pushed off, and within a couple of hours, were well out in the Irish Sea, the fog came in solid. Marion had not mentioned leaving while in Dublin, so I was glad she had decided to hang on till the end. Maybe she was having fun after all.

As we moved south in the soup, we could hear the ferries moving across the sea. Our radar was worth its weight in gold, to be able to see them tracking across and behind us, and not at us. We traveled in the fog all the way down the east side of Ireland, and that night about 2:00 a.m., found me on watch alone. The rest of the crew was sleeping below, and the fog was thick, the wind had died. Suddenly, I heard a whooshing sound near the boat, something big was swimming around the boat and the smell of seaweed was very strong. It must be a whale I thought. I'm both curious and a little concerned. I didn't want this whale to make physical contact with the boat and break the rudder or worse, tip us over. I shined the flashlight out towards the sound, but it was like shinning into a wall, the fog was so thick. Soon he was gone and I didn't know if I should be happy or disappointed.

On August 7, we were at the same latitude as home, 48 degrees 33 minutes north, but in the North Atlantic.

August 8, and we're really cranking out the miles. We didn't trust the auto-pilot to keep us from broaching i.e. turning sideways, so we hand steered. Ben and I took turns, one hour at a time. It was very tiring to keep the boat headed down the waves. We had caught a portion of a gale and lucky for us, a fair wind, we were being thrown south. Alex had been having pains and thought he was seasick. I didn't dare have him up on deck, the boat had so much motion, and there was a danger of being thrown overboard. After each hour at the wheel, we would come down in the cabin and crash right on the floor. Marion stayed awake to be our alarm clock, and woke us when it was time to go up and steer again.

August 9, and the seas were rough. We had the main sail reefed down to the third reef, as far as we can, without taking it down completely, and the staysail set. This is our heavy weather rig and the boat handles well with this setup.

August 10, and I could bake bread, the wind has blown out as we coasted down the shores of Galicia, Spain and Portugal.

August 11, and later in the afternoon, the Portuguese Trades had kicked in and we were blasting down some impressive waves. Ben was steering and I was sitting beside him, while Marion and Alex were below in the cabin. I had the stays'l set and triple reef main. If I would have been steering, I think I would have noticed the tendency for the boat to round up or broach, but Ben wasn't used to the problem it could create. A huge wave came from behind and knocked us sideways, and before Ben could correct the wind had us laid over sliding sideways down the wave. With the boat laid over so far, the rudder didn't steer anymore, as it's at too much of a horizontal now. We lay helpless for what seemed way too long. Maybe we got down in a trough and the wind lost its power on us, anyway we righted and got straightened out again. I realized that we had to drop the main sail altogether, to keep from being pushed around like that again. Once we had just the stays'l up, we rode along safely. Whew, that was close to a disaster.

That evening, we came close to the entrance of Povoa de Varzim, but the fog was thick, too thick to approach the coast. I knew everyone was anxious to get ashore, but it just wasn't safe in the fog, so we turned the boat around into the waves and trimmed the sail, so we would take the waves on the bow, and drifted back slowly. By morning it was clear and fresh, very little wind. We had drifted off shore about 10 miles, but with the motor running, soon we entered the marina and tied up to a vacant slip. I took the passports to the office and checked us in. Soon Ben and Alex had purchased bus tickets for Lisbon, where they had friends to visit, and were gone.

Marion and I spent the next nine days getting the boat ready for winter and having it hauled out. We got placed right alongside the sidewalk, that all the boater's use when coming up from the dock on the way to the showers. While we worked on the boat, we got to say good morning to them all and engage in small talk. It's fun at times, except when there are time constraints. I was rushing to get a lot done before we had to leave, however we did met a lot of interesting sailors that way.

Marion never mentioned leaving more than twice, although I'm sure she thought about it a lot. I was glad she stuck with the trip. At times we needed everyone to help make it a successful trip. We have some good memories of this year's sailing, and luckily I think the bad ones fade somewhat. I like the saying, "If I knew how it would turn out, I could have had more fun."

I thought that was the end of our 2002 boating season, but there were problems on the horizon in a few months.

December 2002, Boat is Damaged in Portugal

In November, I got an e-mail from the mechanic at the marina saying that on November 13, my boat had been struck by the neighboring boat during a storm. His mast had struck my rigging and had broken my mast. Did I want him to take down my mast? I e-mailed back to take the mast down and I would come to see the damage.

On December 3, Terry, our son, and I would travel back to Povoa, to look over the damage and plan what to do next. We got to Povoa, and found the mast in two pieces. The boat that had hit me, sustained no damage. The storm had a lot of rain that softened the ground his stands were sitting on, plus the large canvas covering over the cockpit, caught a lot of wind causing the boat to topple over into my boat. We took off the rigging that had been damaged, and made a list of the parts we needed. When we got home I turned in my cost to his insurance company. They refused to pay and I would have to take them to court. I sure didn't want to get into that, and when I found out that I could repair the mast myself. I dropped the whole matter.

I ordered a new sleeve and some new rigging to fix the damage done that winter. Next year, I planned to just live on the boat and fix the damage. I really needed to paint the top sides too, and the weather in Portugal was good for painting. In Norway, it seemed to rain so often it was hard to find a good time to get it painted. Next year would not be a vacation really, kind of a working vacation instead. We wouldn't spend as much time as usual in Europe and could leave later in the spring.

2003 Six Weeks in Portugal

This summer, I had first planned on fixing the mast and painting the boat and then sailing into the Mediterranean, but it turned out different. I had a huge project to finish in my shop, build a 45-foot barge for the local power company. I had started it during the winter and was working like mad to get it done. We couldn't leave till that was wrapped up. Our daughter Sara and son-in-law John were home from Kansas for the summer and John was helping me finish this project.

It was very late in the evening, and we only had a few hours left to call it done, when it started to rain. We had to leave in the morning, due to plane tickets already bought. This seemed to be a common theme. Every time we leave for the boat, it's a scramble the last few hours. Since I know this, I try to pack weeks ahead of time, so I only have my clothes to throw together, the important stuff like sailing gear and equipment are ready long before the last day.

Before we leave, I called a friend of mine, Henry, to see if he could come over and finish up the last few hours of welding when I was gone. He agreed to do it. John would be there to help him.

July 14, our daughter Mary drove us from Wannaska, Minnesota to Grand Forks, North Dakota where we would start our trip to Portugal via Minneapolis-St. Paul, Amsterdam, and Lisbon, then we would board a north bound bus for the 5-hour ride to the boat in northern Portugal.

We arrived in Lisbon or Lisboa, with the plan to spend a couple of days sightseeing there, before taking the bus to Povoa. Plans are prone to change and since we had delay

122

problems in Minnesota, with one of our flights, we got to Lisbon late in the evening July 17. Our two-day tour of Lisbon now became one day. We arrived at our reserved hotel room in Lisbon around 11:00 p.m. with our bags and jet lag.

By 7:30 a.m., we got up and ate our included breakfast at the hotel. On the way out the door, the hotel manager gave us a warning about the dangers of mugging in the city, one of his customers had recently been mugged, so it was fresh in his mind. We were a long way from Wannaska, where people still leave houses unlocked and keys in their cars. The biggest crime at home, seems to be driving without a seatbelt on. After a long hike to the trolley, we were prepared to sit and rest for a while. We rode the trolley accidentally to the end of the line. We had intended to get off at St. Jorges castle, but missed the stop. Eventually, we found another trolley heading back the other way, and this time got off on the proper stop. We found the castle and toured the grounds. On the way out, I noticed a man making small items for sale. It turned out to be a knot expert, and we had a nice visit with him and bought many of his creations to bring back as gifts.

On the day we were to catch the bus for Povoa, we got a taxi to take us to the station. It wasn't too far, but we had "luggage" and it would have taken a couple of trips. When we got to the station it was crowded, like most bus stations, and we found the spot where the bus would leave from. We shuttled over the bags with the help of a stranger, I gave him a tip. It was a five-hour ride, and when we got to Povoa at 8:00 p.m., I got a chance to use my very limited Portuguese vocabulary. I found a phone and called for a taxi, but I was really not sure I had accomplished this, until the taxi arrived a few minutes later. By hand pointing, English, and a word or two of Portuguese I got the driver going in the right direction, and soon we were at the door of the pensioner, or residential they call it there. It's a kind of hostel. Tony, one of the many Portuguese we had made friends with, but one of the few that could speak English last year, had made reservations for us and I was glad to see the owner knew we were coming and had a room for us. She spoke little to no English and we had trouble in reverse understanding her Portuguese. Evidently she was used to working with other customers challenged by the Portuguese language like us, and got us to our room no problem. I did notice that she could speak out the correct fee we needed to pay in perfect English. After checking into our room and dropping off our bags, we went out for a walk. I was very anxious to see the boat, but Marion didn't want to walk as far as the boat, about a mile away, so we drifted around the town and later came back to our room.

In the morning, after coffee and buns included with the room, we walked to the boat. As we turned the corner into the marina, we spotted *Indian Summer* resting in her cradle. Marion's first remark, "It looks like crap." The 10 months lay-up had not done anything positive to the rusting top sides. It had been rusting ever since we left Bermuda in 2000. I couldn't find anyone to sandblast the boat, so now my plan was to buy a grinder and grind all the rust and paint off.

I was anxious to get to work and grind off all the rust; for two years I had been waiting for this moment. I had the mast to repair also, and had made up a repair kit with splices and a modified spreader bracket at home. One of our pieces of luggage hadn't made it to Povoa, and it had some of my repair parts. I was worried, but later in the day it was delivered.

During our stay in Povoa, we met many Portuguese, Vitor, Paulo, Rego and Rui. There were a lot of other guys around too, but these were the ones who could speak some English. When one of the English speaking fellows would come around and talk with us, it seemed that it attracted many others who would drift in, to ask about us through the interpreters.

We were the official greeters of the day, having been placed at the beginning of the sidewalk, for boaters coming to the bathroom showers from the dock, much to the delight of Marion who loves a good visit. I, on the other hand, was focused on getting projects done before we left in just six weeks.

I went to a local hardware store to buy a grinder. I carried a grinder on the boat, but it was for 110-volts, the standard voltage in Portugal was 220-volts. I bought a high quality grinder and the next day got ready to start grinding off the topside loose paint and rust. As soon as I turned it on, I knew it was defective; it didn't get up to speed. I got Tony to come with me to translate and went back to the store where I had bought it. I had no problem exchanging it for another grinder. I was able to grind about 15 minutes before it too broke down. I really hated to go back with this one broken too, so I took it apart thinking maybe a brush had stuck, but they were OK.

The next day, I went back with Tony to exchange it again. They were a little hesitant to do this a second time, mainly because they only had these two. If I could wait a few days, they could order me a better one, different brand for twice the money. I was anxious to get going, as there was a lot of work to get done in six weeks. So I agreed to wait for the replacement grinder. I could work on other things during that time.

The third grinder arrived, and I finally got a chance to remove the failed paint and rust. I had scrounged around for a broken down scaffolding and duct taped it together. I would grind away a short section at a time, leaving enough time in the day to have Marion treat the rusted area with rust stop, and time for me to get a good two-part primer rolled on, before the evening dew would settle in. It took a week to do this. When everything was primed, I rolled on two coats of top paint. Finally, *Indian Summer* looked good again. We gave the deck a painting too. The deck can be painted while in the water, so it was a bonus to have this done. The deck gets lots of abuse and needs paint every year anyway.

To repair the mast, I used aluminum sleeves made from a short section of the same size mast I had brought from home. When the mast had broken, it just folded the top 12-feet over and crunched five-inches of the mast in the bent area. Carefully sawing, making a squared end on each side of the damaged area was the first step. Next, I inserted the sleeves and drilled and tapped 70, ¼ inch stainless bolts. Then I pulled everything apart, cleaned it and spread a good marine adhesive on the sleeve. I pushed everything together and started installing the ¼ inch bolts. After this was done, we would wait till next year to raise the mast and install the rigging. Part way through this intense boat work, I realized that getting the boat launched and sailing to the Mediterranean, would take more time than we had allowed. I checked with the marina about keeping my boat there another year, it was OK with them. We could relax a bit now and so we spent more time touring around on the bikes I had bought for us.

The motorcycle was too hard to unload, and I hadn't applied for insurance for this summer either, so I never considered taking it out.

Tony had a car and took us around some places too. We saw a food and craft show and ate an interesting meal there, octopus. We had met another Portuguese sailor, Rego, who was building his own boat out of steel. I gave him some of my rigging I was replacing, so later we got invited over for supper and also met his wife. It was very short notice she said, so we had pork-chops, if she would have had more time she would have fixed octopus. I heard later from Marion that she was glad it was short notice.

The summer ended quickly, and we had made plans to take the train from Porto to Madrid. When we were waiting at the station in Porto, there was a track change, and since the message was in Portuguese we missed the train. That meant taking three different trains to get to the same place and some were close connections. It was stressful, and of course we had the maximum baggage to drag from train to train. I'm surprised we made the connections, but we did.

It maybe wasn't the adventure/vacation we had expected, but we did meet some nice folks, and next year we planned to take the boat from Povoa de Varzim in Northern Portugal, to somewhere on the north coast of Northern Spain. We had heard good things about Sada in Galicia, and would try to get some information about it from other sailors, as we sailed north. My plans to continue south from Portugal were scrapped, and I looked forward to exploring the other side of the islands we missed on the way down from Norway. We could work our way back up to Norway in the following years.

2004 Portugal to Sada, Northern Spain

Indian Summer, now had a new paint job plus a reworked mast and we were ready for the sea again. First the launch though. Terry had flown in from Minnesota again, to experience Portugal while we were there, and he would help me as we launched the boat. We had been out of the water for two years now, and after they lowered me into the water I had them keep me in the sling, till I could try out the engine and transmission. It all seemed to work OK, so they let me go. I slid backwards through the water with the transmission in reverse. It was going so smoothly, till I put the gear shift in forward to stop our rearward travel. Nothing happened, we just kept going backwards towards a whole row of boats, and the transmission wouldn't shift. I couldn't stop our boat without the boat shifting, so when we got close to the first tied up boat, I jumped aboard her and tried to push us back. Ever try to stop 14-ton? Well, I didn't stop it, but the fiber glass boat I hit sure did, with a crunch. I had punched a neat hole in the stern; luckily it was above the waterline so no danger of it sinking. My steel boat received a tiny scratch in the paint on the back corner. Now the transmission shifted in forward and we motored over to our slip. To this day, I don't know why it didn't shift. It never missed a shift again, but it took me a long time to gain confidence in it. I contacted the owner of the boat I hit, and he thought 500 dollars would fill the hole alright, I paid him cash.

While Terry was there, we took the boat out in the open water and shifted numerous times, but never could get the transmission to miss shifting again.

After a few more days, we took a trip to Porto, Terry flew home and Marion and I started sailing north. It's tricky going north in those waters, because in the afternoon, the north wind really picks up and creates a sea they call the Portuguese Trades. We couldn't sail against them, so we would leave early in the morning and get to a marina or anchorage, before the waves got too large. We made many stops along the way with adventures in a lot of them.

Baiona was interesting, we spent some time there taking the bicycles off and getting away from the boat. On foot about two miles, seems to be as far as we would go from the boat. The bikes gave us much farther range and we could buy a few things that we could tie on to the bikes. I met a friend Rui from Portugal, there too, as he had sailed up with some of his friends. They had started out about the same time as we did from Portugal, but partway their boat had sprung a leak, only a broken hose or gasket, but a little frightening for them. They had to be pulled in to get it fixed. Baiona has some history, as it is the first place that one of the Columbus boats returned, to announce that they had discovered the new world, not knowing the Indians of North America knew about all it all the time. A big sign near the marina, advertises their route to and from the new world. One day we just packed a lunch, and our day tent, and went hiking along the shore. When we found a nice place to pitch the tent, we just relaxed for the rest of the day. We could see a group of islands to the north and made plans to stop there when we left.

A few days, later when we stopped at those islands we went ashore for a walk on the long sandy beach. As we walked along we met three college age girls, and I noticed they had such big smiles as we passed by them. After they were out of hearing, Marion said, "Did you see that?" "See what?" I asked. "Those girls were topless." This is why it's so handy to have another pair of eyes with you, they notice things that are missed. This island had some huge hills. In Minnesota, we would call them mountains, with a road to the top of one. We walked to the top and got a fine view of the sea and surroundings. When we are that far away from the boat, I get a little nervous. Anchors can drag with the shifting currents, but from that high up I could see *Indian Summer,* lying calmly to her anchor.

One morning, fishermen came around our boat and began dropping their nets, I think they were fishing for octopus and it was interesting to watch them. It was a pleasant spot to hang out in, and we only had two or three boats for neighbors, lots of room to ourselves. I hated to leave.

Next port was Cambados in the Ria de Arosa. Close to the harbor, were many mussel rafts and it was hard to see a way in, so we just hung out waiting for a fishing boat to follow in. Soon, one did come and we dropped in behind him. He went into an enclosed breakwater and over to a group of other fishing boats. We knew we couldn't tie up in the fishing boat slips; we would be chased out, so we found a corner in the harbor to anchor in, out of the traffic lane.

We stayed on the boat for a few hours to make sure no one cared if we were there, no one came, so later we went into town. In town, there was a Celtic celebration going on with music and vendors. The next day, a French sailboat came in and motored into one of the fishing boat slips. He wasn't there long before he was told to move, they had him tied up behind some docks and later at low tide I saw him leaning over some, he had settled on the bottom.

The next marina we visited was Vilagarcia, not very far away and in the same Ria de Arosa, no Portugese Trades to worry about in there. When we came into the marina, the open slip they gave us was next to the French boat we saw in Cambados. They said they had noticed us at Cambados, anchored in the corner of the harbor and commented that they heard we were part of the Celtic celebration program. "Who told you that?" we asked. Well, when they had come into the harbor at Cambados, and asked about anchoring in the corner where we were, they were told that was only for people taking part in the celebration. Glad we didn't ask around while we were in Cambados, we would have had to move too.

While in Vilagarcia we took the train north to Santiago de Compostela. It has a huge cathedral that is built over the bones of the disciple St. James, we were told. St. James had brought Christianity to the Iberian Peninsula, and later after he was beheaded in 44 AD, his bones were returned to Compostela. The original building was destroyed, but in 1075 the existing one was started and finished in 1211. For anyone familiar with the Bible, you could find carvings of a lot of biblical figures, throughout the building inside and out. We spent all day wandering around town buying a few trinkets from some street vendor's. We returned to Vilagarcia the same day by train.

The next day, there was a huge navy ship unloading passengers and vehicles. I asked what was going on, and they told us that a large group of kids had taken the ship to Mexico, Southern Spain and Portugal and were now just returning home. They had a big program outside for them, complete with costume dancers, all very entertaining. While walking around the town, we noticed a flier advertising a bacalhoe or cod meal in an old looking tin building. We like to try new things so we went in. There were a few choices of prepared bacalhoe to choose from, with a bottle of wine. We saw two sizes of wine bottles, small and a normal size. I thought the director of the meal knew we wanted two small bottles, but we got two large ones. We felt a little foolish carrying our meal to the table each carrying a big bottle of wine. We hid one bottle in a bag on the floor. Crazy Americans. The cod was excellent.

After Vilagarcia, we stopped in Muros, Cape Finisterre, Laxe and finally Sada. In Muros, we went ashore with a couple of cans to fill with diesel. There was an older gentleman watching us from the shore, complete with his sea cap on. He couldn't speak any English, but he saw we were after fuel. He motioned that he could drive us to the nearest station, which he did and when I offered to pay him, he refused to be paid. He did worry us some the way he drove, so cautious that we thought either he didn't have a license or it wasn't his car. Later, he invited us into his house across the street, and showed us his certificate indicating he had at one time held a captains license. Next to his license, he had placed a picture of our boat I had given him earlier. He always wore a seaman's cap and looked like he had spent a lot of time on the water, probably as a fisherman we thought. We noticed an older woman in the house that could have been his mother or sister. We missed so much when we couldn't speak the local language.

While in Finisterre harbor, after we anchored, we took the skiff for a ride back along the coast, to explore some caves we had noticed coming in. At low tide, we could bring the skiff right up to the mouth of one of the caves to explore it. I hadn't brought along a flashlight, so we didn't go in farther than we could see. Also, in Finisterre harbor, we had taken the skiff into town and spent some time walking around and met some folks from the states, but when we got back to the skiff, we found it hanging by its dock lines, the tide had went out. We hadn't meant to be gone so long, so I hadn't allowed for the tide drop. I quickly lowered it down, but the outboard motor was now stuck in the mud, so I couldn't drag it around to us, and the water and mud was too filthy to walk in. The only thing we could do, was go back uptown and wait a few hours for the tide to come in.

When we left Finisterre, the next port was Laxe, it was late in the day so we went to bed without going ashore. In the morning, I could tell we were at the end of our vacation/adventure, because, when I asked Marion if she wanted to go ashore and see a 12th century church advertised in our guide, she just rolled over in the bunk and said, "No, I've seen five already." Later we pulled up the anchor and left without going ashore to explore.

Next stop was Sada, where we had a little trouble communicating, since our Spanish wasn't what it should have been, but we managed through sign language. What we wanted was a place to tie up and then a spot to get hauled out for the coming winter months. Soon we were on the way home, another cruising season done. We hadn't traveled very far, about 200-miles, but we stopped at 11 ports and saw some interesting sights. It was worth it. But like I've always said, "You can only have so much fun before it's not fun anymore." It was time to go home.

2005 Sada to Kilrush, Ireland

In the beginning, our plans were to sail *Indian Summer,* from her winter berth near La Coruna, Spain, to the western coast of Ireland, with stops in France, England and Ireland. While in England, we would leave the boat at a marina, and fly to Norway for a short visit again with some of Marion's relatives in Norway. One of our daughters, Mary, and son, Terry would fly to Norway and meet us there. After a week of visiting, Mary would fly home after visiting MayBritt, a former school friend who had moved back to Norway, and Terry would come back to the boat with us and sail to Ireland. He had a return flight from Dublin. We had a specific time to get him somewhere in Ireland in time, so he can take the bus or train to Dublin airport.

The adventure would start June 7, three days after our youngest daughter's marriage and end August 21, with a flight home from Madrid, Spain. Since there are variables that change with time, we have to keep an open mind and be willing to change our plans to adapt. Traveling by sailboat means we are dependent on weather conditions, so we are never positive of our arrival time or even a specific port. Sometimes we are just happy to arrive---sometime, anywhere, and safely. Mary has described our trips as Vacation Boot Camp. There might be a little truth to it too. I say, that not all adventurers can be vacations.

On June 10, we arrived in Sada, Spain where we had left *Indian Summer,* 10 months before. We had flown from Grand Forks, North Dakota, to Minneapolis, to Amsterdam, to Madrid, to La Coruna and a bus from La Coruna to Sada. We did have a full day to spend in Madrid, so we went to the Prado, had a nice lunch and did some hiking around.

The next day, we flew over to La Coruna and got a local bus to Sada. Sada, is an old fishing village that now attracts vacationers and sailors from Wannaska. From the bus stop, we had a mile walk to the boat. We had two rolling bags filled with boating gear and provisions for the summer. We hooked them up in tandem that I pulled, and Marion pulled her airline carryon bag. When we got to the boat everything looked fine, actually she looked great. The last two summers we had spent in Portugal, gave us nice weather for painting, so we made use of it. We had spent a lot of time painting the hull and deck.

Scrounging a ladder from the marina, I climbed on deck. Things were dirty, but not greasy like before in Portugal, where there are textile factories near the marina, creating smog that settled on the deck. Anxious to get inside, I quickly untied the storm boards, unlocked and slid back the hatch. The cabin air didn't seem bad, not too musty. Next, I lifted out the floorboard over the bilge and saw it was full of water. I was afraid this would happen. The sail locker hatch had rotted in one corner, and over the past 10 months, had let in rain water which had run into the bilge. It had a long way to go before it filled the bilge, and soaked any gear, but I hate having water in the boat. My first chore was to bail it out. Later, we hauled out all the sailing gear and the two bikes. Then brought in our luggage; our vacation boot camp had begun.

During the next 15 days, we worked hard to complete a list of boat projects. As the seasons pass, things deteriorate and become unsafe. It is always good to stay connected to the boat and all her gear; it's much easier to stop some things that are beginning to fail. I replaced the prop shaft seal, that had been leaking the previous summer, relocated the radar antenna on the more stable generator mast, replaced the wood covering the steering pedestal, and replaced the wood sail locker hatch that had let water leak in. Marion cleaned and painted the cockpit floor and cabin area. I also found a marine store that could order me a life raft. I had tried to get one last year, but twice there was a problem and I had to cancel. I bought Marion a self-inflating life vest too. She was starting to get concerned at this point. Why a life raft and life vest this summer?

We did take time to attend a St. John festival, spend a day at the beach, visit a school musical program, and go for walks in the evenings. Many evenings we would spend sitting in the cockpit after our workday was over, listening to the foreign sounds of being in another country, while we ate olives and drank their very reasonable price wine. Could it get any better?

On June 22, we were set back in the water and it was great to be afloat again. We motored over to an open slip, and spent the next four days putting things away, and collecting extra stores for the trip.

We met some interesting sailing folks in Sada, some Americans, Pat and Jack on *Woosh,* and some English ones, Dave and Susan on *Stella*. Dave and Susan were going to start an around the world cruise. We got invited over for visits sometimes too.

It was here that we met a New Zealander, what a

character. My notes don't record his name, so I'll just call him Ben. What attracted us to him was his boat; it was made of steel like ours. Most boats have fiberglass as their main construction, due to easier maintenance, but steel has them all beat for its strength. Well, when we saw this boat a little ways down the dock from us, we had to meet him. Ben had quite a story to tell. He had bought the unfinished steel hull in Ireland, and spent a year finishing it out. He was going to sail it back to New Zealand, and got a friend to join him. While crossing the Bay of Biscay, his friend thought he was having a heart attack and insisted that Ben call for his evacuation.

A ship responded and his friend was too sick to try taking the skiff across to the ship, he wanted Ben to come alongside the ship. It's very risky to transfer people from a small boat to a ship, even when they aren't injured. Knowing it would wreck his spreaders and make the mast fall, over he did it anyway to save his friend's life. They did get him aboard the ship, and as expected smashed the rigging by banging into the side of the ship. Soon after the ship left, the mast fell into the sea.

Ben got to Sada by motoring, and had been there a month already. By luck, he found a used mast at the marina and made it fit his boat. He was about ready to leave, about the time we met him. He told us that his friend had called him to say that it was only stress and not a heart attack; he wanted to join him again. I guess Ben thought he had had enough of him and said he would rather sail alone now.

The departure morning was not what I had hoped for. An overcast sky with a light drizzle, was coming down with a wind from the north. This would bring a swell into the Ria, that we will have to motor through, and it will get a little splashy, as *Indian Summer* raises and plunges into it. Marion is not a morning person and this was not helping her get enthused about leaving Sada.

The weather had been warm and sunny the past few days, after we had been lifted from our storage cradle and set in the water, however, it had taken us a few days to put things away and collect our stores for the voyage to Ireland via England, and now the weather had changed. Even though we had been in Sada for two weeks preparing to leave, Marion could still find reasons for not leaving port. We had already delayed departure by one day and now I was anxious to leave. Departure is always tricky. There are always reasons to stay another day, and another day, but there are times when I think it's important to stick with the plan. Of course it's always good to have a plan B too, and I felt we could always return or anchor out, if things looked too bad.

Jack, an American boater, who with his wife Pat had just sailed into Sada a few days earlier, came over to help push us off. He had a copy of the latest weather forecast for our area, and it looked alright from what I could make out. Of course, I can't read much of Spanish, but have studied enough to recognize the word for gale, and I didn't see it on the page he gave me. I appreciated his help in getting away from the dock. I was still trying to build up my confidence in the engine machinery, after the incident last year, when the transmission refused to go into forward, after backing out of the lift out slip in Portugal. It's like having your brakes fail. The problem was, that I never could find the reason it failed and have always been waiting for the other shoe to drop. However, this time all went smoothly, the transmission went into reverse, we slid out of the slip and then back into forward with a satisfying clunk, and at 7:15, headed out of the harbor.

When we had cleared the jetty, we could feel *Indian Summer* rising and falling to the swell. Marion, a confessed fair weather sailor, was still expressing her negative opinion of my decision to leave in the rain as we motored out. However, she stayed at the helm while I cleared up the deck of dock lines and fenders. We set the main sail about an hour later to help out the engine and steady the boat. The wind was too far forward to use the headsail. That would have given us more speed and let us shut down the engine. At least with the main set, the wind will hold the boat over some and prevent us from rolling side to side. Our next port would be Cedeiro, about 35-miles away to the east. We had heard from Jack and Pat that it was a nice place to visit, so our hopes were up.

It was good to be free of land once more, and have the feel of the ocean swell beneath our feet. *Indian Summer,* is a strong boat and we have been through some rough water together, so I have confidence in her ability to take care of us, less so in her machinery though.

It's important that I should keep a vigilant eye out for anything unusual. That's one reason I hate running the engine, as there are many more mechanical items to keep watch on, plus the smell of diesel, the noise of the engine blocking out the sounds of wind on the sails, and the water off the hull; then of course the cost of $4.00 a gallon fuel. We came out of the Betanzos Ria, and once again spotted the ancient Roman lighthouse, the Tower of Hercules, to the west of us. It had been a welcome sight last year, when coming along the coast, as we knew our destination for the end of the summer was close at hand.

However, now we turned right and headed northeast keeping about five miles off the coast. The coast line is mountainous with some shallow bays cut in. This would be a poor place to have trouble in a storm; the waves crashing against the rocks are very unforgiving to a boat adrift. I'm thankful to have both sails and engine working together. We had a foul current close to shore, but since we weren't going very far before running in, we kept closer to the cliffs than I normally would have. We had a good idea of the way into Cedeiro, and a few hours later we came into the bay, bypassing some rocks on the way with no problem. At 2:30 in the afternoon, we set the anchor in 30-feet of water ¼ mile from shore, and away from other anchored boats. We have a nine foot inflatable with a ten horsepower outboard engine, so getting to and from shore is no problem.

Cedeiro is a well-protected harbor with a large bay. There are no facilities for pleasure boaters here, but that is OK for us. We only need a place to beach our skiff and collect fresh water. We are here to explore and don't need to be catered to. It is our custom while sailing to different ports, to savor the experience, so now we were in no special hurry to get ashore. After the anchor is set and the deck cleaned up, we can relax in the cockpit while looking over the area.

It's fun to formulate questions about different buildings and structures we see from our position. They always look so fascinating and we are anxious to explore them, but we know when we do, they will lose some of their magic, we will wait till tomorrow to begin. The evening is pleasant as we watch the sunset and later the shore lights come on. When we go to bed, we are gently rocked to sleep; some days can be so satisfying.

I was up early this morning to finish up a project I had been working on. I was lacing on some netting to the forward deck, to prevent the sails from slipping into the sea when they are lowered. When there are only two of us to run the boat, one must be at the helm, Marion, and one at the mast to run the halyards, me. When the sails are dropped, there is a minute or two before I can get at them to tie them up. Sometimes, when it's rough, we can get a wave that washes over the deck before I can get to the sails, and then it's difficult to drag them back aboard. The netting will keep them on deck till I can tie them down.

When the netting project was finished, we got ready to go ashore. The inflatable is lowered from its position on the foredeck, and the outboard lifted over from the cockpit railing into the boat and onto the transom. We carried with, an empty water container, in case we saw some handy fresh water tap. Motoring up to shore, we landed at a boat ramp and set the retractable skiff wheels down. We stepped ashore and pulled the boat up the ramp on its wheels.

We did find a fresh water tap close to the boat ramp, so we filled our portable jugs there. It was a nice walk to town and we stopped to visit with some trailer campers from England, on the way. We found a restaurant to have lunch and it sure had an interesting restroom configuration, instead of a toilet, there was a foot-print to show where to stand and a hole in the floor. This town had a river running right though it, and at high water it was very pretty, and at low water not so much.

The next day, we decided to hike to a lighthouse that was straight across from our anchored boat, about one-half-mile across. The shore didn't look very inviting, but we had heard of a nice path along the bay, starting about two miles away from the boat and going right up to the lighthouse. We packed a lunch in our backpacks and started out in the skiff. We beached it close to the beginning of the path to the lighthouse and started out. They were many eucalyptus trees on the way that gave off a nice smell. When we reached the lighthouse, we could see our boat lying across from us, so I could relax knowing it was safe. We sat down and had our coffee and lunch.

We hiked further down the path a little later and saw another place to motor over to with the skiff, there were a lot of sandbars at low tide and some kids where playing on them. We would have to check it out later. We hiked on back to the skiff and started back to the boat.

The sun was setting and it was close to the direction we were headed. I couldn't see our boat, but thought it was just me, till Marion said, "Do you see our boat?" Now that got me worried thinking it had floated away while we were out hiking. It took a few minutes before we could make it out, due to the sun reflecting on the water and hiding the boat.

The next day, being nice also, we took the skiff over to the other spot we noticed yesterday with the sandbars. We spent some time wading around in the shallow, warm water, and watching the tide come in and cover up the sandbars again. We had brought lunch along, so had our picnic there too.

The next port we went to was Carino. It was a well-protected bay with a few boats anchored there. An English man was anchored a little forward of us and we talked with him, as we motored in with the skiff one day. We had read in our sailing instructions, that this harbor has a lot of foul cables that would snag our anchor, so we put a trip line on ours before dropping it.

One day while we were hanging out on the boat, the English man came over to ask for some help in freeing his anchor, it was snagged on something on the bottom and he couldn't pull it up. I went over to see what I could do. I think we slipped a ring of some sort over his anchor line and attached another line to this ring and let it slide down the anchor line. Then by pulling up, we were able to back the anchor out from whatever it had snagged on. He was happy to be free and reset his anchor in a better spot. I think he had been caught there for a while trying to get free. He had taken some time off work, or for some reason, had five years to sail and was in no hurry to go anywhere, but I had the feeling he was intimidated by sailing alone. He had a scare coming into Carino as his motor had quit at a bad time, while he was motoring along the rocky cliffs, and he was lucky to sail out of the situation without wrecking his boat.

This town had a nice beach, and one day as we motored in, a group of five or six young kids saw us and came running down to the landing. I really didn't want to have them tampering with our skiff when were gone, so I turned and went over to another spot, which they quickly ran to also. I gave up and beached right in front of them. They spoke no English, but I think they sensed Marion was a teacher and flocked around her. I got a nice group picture of all of them.

Marion is a rock or pebble collector. One day, while

she was walking the beach looking for interesting rocks, an elderly man came by. Seeing her picking up pebbles, he started helping her by finding some more for her. He couldn't speak a word of English and of course we are just as bad in Spanish, but I did show him our boat in the harbor.

In this town, we found out about a camping music celebration going on in a neighboring town, so we found a bus heading that way. When we got there, we did find a mob of people camped out and a lot of activity, but there seemed to be a lot of underage drinking going on. We felt a little old for this festival anyway. We found another bus to take us back to the boat. We had only one more stop to make before striking out across the Bay of Biscay, this was Viveiro, Galacia.

July 13, Viveiro, we planned to leave Viveiro tomorrow for Falmouth, England, a distance of 400 nautical miles of open ocean sailing across the Bay of Biscay. With a favorable wind, we can cover between 100 to 130-miles in a 24-hour period. That means the best we could do it in, would be three to four days, then factor in say 1/3 of the time not favorable wind, so, add two more days, and maybe one day of no wind, so that means seven days on the outside. So today we will water and fuel the boat, pick up final groceries, and e-mail friends and relatives.

We loaded up the three jerry cans and motored into the river that cuts into the town. There we found diesel stored in jugs at a yacht basin, which we transferred to our jugs. While I was doing this, Marion went to the Hiperstore to get groceries. I finished with the fuel before she got back, so I walked to the store to help carry things back. We had a heavy load going back to the boat. We traveled slowly with our cargo, since it was still windy and the harbor was bumpy. We got the stores off loaded and got ready to go back to shore, with water jugs, and a final trip to the e-mail café.

I had stopped the outboard in gear when approaching the boat earlier, and forgot to put it in neutral again. Marion had her life jacket on as usual, and was standing up in the skiff, holding onto the boat to keep us from drifting, until I had the outboard started. I gave a mighty pull on the starting rope. The engine started and immediately lunged forward, since it was still in gear, sending Marion falling into me. It's considered a bad omen to have anything fall into the sea before a voyage and I think that would include the first mate. Luckily, the engine stalled and we both stayed aboard. However, the air was a bit heavy on the way in.

We did get to shore without further incident and pulled the boat well up on shore. We got to the e-mail café and sent off our Northern Spain letter.

Marion writes: *Dear Friends and Family,*
Since leaving Sada a couple of weeks ago, we are in our third port. We've stayed about a week at each place. We have been anchoring in the harbors or off the beach, and using the rubber raft to go ashore. We haven't talked to many people since leaving Sada, except for an English sailor we met at the last Harbor. One day, we took a bus to another town for a music event and talked to some English people there. There were a lot of people there, and it was an adventure going on the bus, as we weren't sure about the schedule.
We have decided to bypass France and sail directly to Falmouth, England, on the southwest tip of England. We plan to leave tomorrow, so we have stocked up on fuel, groceries and water. The wind isn't in the best direction for us, but we are used to that. The wind hasn't changed in the

last two weeks. That's Murphy's law of sailing, where ever you're going, that's where the wind is coming from. Some of the forecast looks good. Please pray for our safety and the winds to be in the right direction and the right speed. We hope to arrive in England by Monday at the earliest, or Wednesday at the latest. Please keep in touch. We enjoy hearing from you. Jerry and Marion.

By the time we left the café it was 11:00 in the evening, and I was anxious to get back to the skiff. I have been fooled by the tides before, and twice it has floated off the beach, but saved by someone who happened to be there and pulled it back to shore. Coming from Minnesota, and not used to tides it seems foolish to haul the skiff so far from the water, but I'm learning. Besides, I don't like leaving it unprotected and unlocked in the dark, and I still had water jugs to fill. We found our way back to the beach, and Marion tried calling a few people as we still had time left on the card, but most were not home, she did reach Melissa, our niece, at home though. We loaded in the water and pushed off, heading out into the dark harbor. Since I hadn't planned on returning in the dark, I had neglected to leave a lantern lit in the cockpit. Small fish jumped out of the water in front of us, as we slowly motored out in the direction of our boat. We passed a few anchored boats and then the dark shape of *Indian Summer* came into view, and soon we were alongside. After offloading the stores, we went to bed too tired to put anything away, besides we didn't want to use any battery power for lights.

In the morning we would load the skiff and engine and put away the stores. We went to sleep under the open hatch, the wind had gone down and it was very pleasant out, tomorrow would be a big day for us and I was anxious to get moving again. July 14, Vivero, today we will leave for southern England. I had decided to pass on stopping in France. We got up at first light to start putting things away from the night before. I got the skiff ready to load, first, was to lift off the motor, we have a system that makes it easy and safe. Marion stands in the cockpit and lifts the lower end of the outboard. It also acts as a safety rope in case I slip and the engine goes over the side. As Marion lifts one end, I stood in the raft and lift the head part of the motor. We got the motor up and swung into the cockpit in a couple of seconds. Then I climbed aboard and stood the motor up and walked it over to the railing, where we have a mounting bracket and fastened it on. Then I crawled back on to the skiff and pulled it forward and hand Marion the painter. Then with both of us standing on the deck, we begin pulling the boat sideways, to the top of the railing and roll it over onto the foredeck where it is tied down on the four corners. By 9:30 we had everything put away.

Marion motored us up to a position right above the anchor, where I cleated off the chain and let the ocean pull the anchor from the mud. The swell lifts the boat and the boat lifts the anchor from the mud. Then it's heave ho on the 45-pound anchor and anchor chain, till it's raised to the surface and clanked into place. But as soon as the anchor is free of the bottom, I give Marion the signal to begin moving out of the harbor. Marion steered us out of the harbor and into the open ocean, while I got the deck cleaned up of lines and prepared to make sail.

When we cleared the Ria, we found the winds NW force three or four. Since our course was 020 degrees, we could work with this wind. We reefed the main once and hauled up the jib. Our speed reached six knots plus, the best we could hope for. After connecting the auto pilot, we found she wouldn't steer herself, but kept rounding up or turning into the wind where she stopped sailing. I figured that there was too much weather helm, so I reefed the main once more and the autopilot began to work with no reduction in speed. The seas were a bit bumpy and sloppy at times when we got too close to the wind and met the waves more head on, but we had good speed all day and into the night. At four in the afternoon, I laid down on the settee for a cat nap and slept till six, while Marion stayed on watch. Then after I got up she made supper. Marion went to bed and was up again at 3:00 a.m. and stayed on watch till 6:00 while I slept.

While at sea, I have a difficult time thinking about anything other than the boat and the passage. If there is trouble coming, I like to be ready for it and so I keep looking for developing problems. I look at the sails, sheets, and halyards for chaffing, the auto pilot for any loose hardware, and every 15 minutes a complete check of the horizon for any shipping traffic. Down below deck, there is the bilge to check for any water coming in, any loose gear that has come adrift. If the engine is running, I check to make sure it has oil and not overheating, that the generator is charging, how much fuel is left, notice any unusual vibration that would indicate a worn shaft bearing or zincs coming loose from the shaft, or maybe the shaft has picked up a stray rope and wrapped it around the prop. These are a few of the things I continually look at.

When the weather was nice we did play some cards up on deck or plenty of time to talk, and Marion found some time to read and work on a quilt sewing project. I still have my ham radio on board, so we tune into the BBC for news. Of course, anytime there is a ship or small craft spotted, we get out the binoculars to look them over. The navtex is checked regularly for any change in the weather forecast or special bulletins and our position plotted every 24 hours. At noon on the second day out, we had covered 116 miles and met three sailboats during the morning. The seas had calmed down and the sky was sunny and clear. During the night, the wind ceased completely, so we began running the engine. The wind came back light, a little later, so we tried sailing, but by noon it was hopeless, so we motored the rest of the day. For a few hours in the evening we had wind again so the engine got a break. When rounding the corner of France we must avoid the traffic separation zones, which are lanes of opposite traffic used by shipping in congested areas. Ships like to travel the shortest distance between ports, and this makes certain areas more prone to collision, sort of an intersection at sea. We were close enough to them that we had many ships to look out for. Once we cleared them, we worked our way into the English Channel.

During the night, there was enough traffic to keep us alert. It actually is a good thing to see lights at sea, because that tells us that we are not sailing in fog and unable to see an approaching ship. If there is a question, I can turn on the radar to get a better picture of our area. We can observe a distance of 16 miles, but actually eight miles or closer, gives a more accurate picture for us since our radar antenna is only 12-feet above the surface.

We came into Falmouth on Monday the 18. The last 9 ½ hours were rough, rain and windy. On entering the harbor, we encountered the most sail craft I've seen in one place. It was very windy and the local sailing craft were out in force, darting in and out of our path. We were very tired and just wanted to get to an anchorage so we could rest.

We came up to the moorings and since we weren't really sure which ones were for visitors, we planned to take an open one and go ashore and ask. We located an open one on the edge of the moorings, so we slowly came up to it. We had not picked up a mooring before, and had nothing other than a boat stick with a peg on the end. I was somehow thinking I could hold on to it while I passed a line through the loop. I managed to get hold of the mooring first try, but when Marion put the transmission in neutral, the wind was too strong for me to hold on and we slipped away. Each time we came up to the mooring, we learned something, mostly what didn't work. By the fifth time we had a good idea what to do, having tried all the other possibilities. This time, I brought the boat up to the mooring and by shifting the transmission in and out of gear, we could stay in one place for a while. Marion managed to get a line through the loop on the mooring. I rushed forward to help secure it to the boat. Luckily for the boats tied up nearby, their occupants had some entertainment for a while.

Needless to say, it was good to be tied down after the five day run up from Spain. I enjoyed the moment by collapsing on the settee in the cabin and freeing my mind of all the looming problems that I had been thinking of for the past five days. We had our share of excitement for the day, and as usual decided to go ashore in the morning. For now, we would just enjoy the stress free evening in a protected harbor, attached firmly to the sea bottom.

In the morning, after I had furled the sails properly and straightened up the deck, we were getting ready to go ashore. I was preparing our skiff, when a small training sailboat made a quick tack behind us and plopped one of the two sailors overboard. His partner had drifted out of reach to retrieve him. I hollered over to him if I should come pick him up, "Oh no, I'm learning," he said. In the meantime, his partner had made a circle and sailed up to him to fish him out.

A short time later, a customs boat came along side to check our papers. All was in order and we had a nice visit with them. Then three fellows came by in their skiff and stopped to say hello. They had noticed our American flag and they were from Michigan. They would be heading down to Portugal the next day.

When we got ashore later, we found that we had selected a resident's mooring and had to move pronto. We motored back to the boat, taking a tour through the visitor moorings and found them all taken. We elected to anchor and wait for a visitor mooring to open up. If we had noticed the anchored boats in the first place, we would have just anchored there when we first got in. It's difficult to come into a strange harbor and have to sort things out while tired. It was much easier to leave the mooring than attach to it. We came forward a bit with help of the engine, to take the pressure off the line, caused by the wind pushing the boat back. I untied the line and let her slip through the loop we fought so hard to tie too. We drifted back and out of the mooring. Swinging around we motored over to the anchorage and dropped the hook and let the wind take us back a ways, before cinching the rode and setting the anchor. I let out a little more line to make sure the tide wouldn't lift us up and release the anchor.

The two problems with anchoring here; are the need to leave if a big ship comes into port, as they need this space to come into the dock, also, when you anchor, there are situations that can break the anchor free and set you adrift. I'm forever trying to catch a glimpse of the boat while we are ashore, ready to dash out, if it looks like it has moved from our anchoring spot. I can never really relax when we are anchored and I'm ashore.

It was evening before we were able to come to shore and inspect the town. Marion found her favorite store, a charity shop, or as we call them here, second hand stores. The more we walked the more charity shops we found. Falmouth was made for Marion. Well, I was also interested in the Cornwall Maritime Museum, and we quickly had the next day worked out. I would tour the museum, Marion would visit as many second hand shops as daylight would allow.

Before we had walked very far, we gave Sara and John a call to say we had survived the crossing of the Bay of Biscay, and were now ashore again trading one danger for another. Our stay in Falmouth was interesting. We had eight days there to explore, before taking a bus to London and a flight over to Norway to visit Marion's relatives. Marion sure liked that town. I think we counted 11 thrift shops there. Falmouth also has an interesting marine history and some good marine shops. It was fun to be there for a while exploring, but soon it was time to go up to London via the bus.

We found a good hostel to stay at in London and toured around the city, some on a double decker bus. We also took the train out to Greenwich to see the prime meridian, Harrison's clocks that made longitude sailing possible, and toured the Cutty Sark.

We had trouble getting into museums, as there had just been a bombing a few weeks ago. We couldn't leave our backpacks in the cloak room and couldn't take them with us in the museum.

After London, we flew to Bergen, where we met Terry and Mary at the airport. They had flown in from Minneapolis. Marion's relatives were there to get us. We had such a good time and Mikal was still feeling well enough to take us around. He had a terminal illness and it was one of the reasons for our visit now. The time to go came much too fast, and soon we were at the airport saying our goodbyes. It was especially hard to leave Mikal knowing that we probably would not see him again.

Mary left from Bergen to visit her friend in Oslo, before going back home to Minnesota.

Terry flew back to London and rode the bus back to Falmouth with us. We left Falmouth, next stop Penzance. Marion flushed out another thrift store there before we sailed over to St. Michael's Mount. It's an island at high tide and at low tide, a bar is exposed so we could walk from the mainland to the mount on the sandbar.

After leaving St. Michael's, we sailed between the Scilly Islands and the mainland, then across the Irish Sea. We were headed for the Shannon River on the west side of Ireland. However, when we got close enough to get a weather forecast on VHF radio, we heard of a strong wind heading our way, so we ducked into Union Bay to wait it out. Terry had return flight tickets from Dublin and we could drop him off there, if the bad weather hung on for a while. We did walk around the town and had a meal at a pub, but soon the winds were favorable to go, so we all left again. There were light winds up the west side. Soon, after entering the Shannon River, on August 16· we found a bay to anchor in.

The chart showed a castle on the shore and sure enough there it was, like a silo from home complete with cattle grazing around it. We took the skiff ashore to inspect it, and found a sign stating that it was built in 1480 and was called the Carrigaholt Castle. We were not able to go inside, but it was well preserved. It's a rectangular construction of five stories high. The information says the last inhabitance were the Burtons in late 19th century. At one time the inhabitances of the castle were under siege, and after a while were promised safe passage if they would surrender. They came out, surrendered, and were promptly killed.

The next day, we motored and sailed up the river about seven miles, to a town called Kilrush. It was controlled by a lock that would keep only high water in the lagoon. We waited for high water and the lock master to open for us. We found a spot to tie up and arranged to be hauled out and stored for the winter. Terry caught a bus in town and made it to Dublin in time to make his flight home. We would leave as soon as the boat was winterized and all the gear taken down and stored in the cabin. It looked like a nice place to hang out. The yard was really a working yard and they didn't mind us working on the boat either. So ends 2005, a very good year of cruising.

2006 A Non-Cruising Summer

This summer we thought it would be a good idea to spend some time just riding the motorcycle around Ireland. After all, we weren't really trying to get anywhere, just enjoying the summer.

We arrived in Ireland on the 25th of July, by way of Dublin and on to Shannon, which is much closer to Kilrush, where we have the boat stored. We found a hostel in Kilrush to spend the first night, as the boat is always so packed with sailing gear for the winter; it is hard to find a place to lie down. After checking into the hostel, I walked down to the boat a few blocks away to see how it weathered. The boat had stayed dry, but was a little musty smelling from being locked up for so many months.

In the next few days, we worked on clearing out the boat and cleaning it up for our cabin for the summer. I also made plans to get the bike out of the cabin, no small feat either. It required making a ramp up from the cabin floor to the cockpit, about a four-foot lift. After I had a plank down for the ramp, I positioned the boom over the main hatch and attached the mainsheet pulley system from the boom to the motorcycle. The motorcycle consisted of the frame, the motor and the rear tire. All the other parts where stored in nooks and crannies around the boat. As I pulled on the mainsheet, the motorcycle would slowly roll up the ramp, while I kept it from tipping over. Once we got it to the cockpit, I had to wait till the next day, before a construction worker who had agreed to come over with his forklift after closing time, and lift it down from the cockpit, a drop of nine

155

feet. Once on the ground, I assembled the parts and soon had a living, breathing motorcycle on Ireland soil.

We toured many places that summer, some boot sales, i.e. flea market for Marion, some castles, and one weekend we loaded up the bike with tent and sleeping bags, and biked to a neighboring town where there was a musical theme going on. It's one of the advantages of hanging out for a while and having a set of wheels to get around in. We did camp out that night, but since we had picked a spot so close to the ocean, it got a little cold. We had seen a lot of the festival the first day, and after spending part of the next day there, we decided to leave. The forecast for the next day was rain and we would rather spend it in the warm cabin of the boat, than on the back of a motorcycle.

I had many little projects to work on through the summer and seemed to be busy every day. Marion and I met a nice couple on another sailboat, Jan and Jasna, who were liveaboards year around, and during the summer months he captained a fishing boat. Jan invited me along to help steer the fishing boat out to the fishing grounds about 15 or 20 miles out, while he tended to other things and hobnobbed with the customers. I helped the fishermen get their rods hooked up, and then could fish if I wanted. There was always lots of fish to bring home, mainly Pollack and Mackerel.

Sometimes we got invited over to Jan and Jasna's boat for supper and he was quite a chef and no wonder because one time he had run a restaurant. He had been a diesel mechanic and a women's hairstylist too. Jan was a man with many talents. Jasna worked as a private secretary in town and had been a fish monger at one time. She sure knew how to clean fish efficiently. We were so lucky to have met them.

They are the kind of people that make voyaging so interesting. That they were living on a steel sailboat made them instant friends with us.

We took another motorcycle tour to Limerick that was interesting. We had to take a ferry across the Shannon River at Killimer, and then a nice ride to Limerick. Before Limerick, we made a stop in Foynes to look at a seaplane museum, where they had a mock-up of a transatlantic terminal and a partial display of a seaplane cabin. It was here, just before the start of World War II, that the first passenger planes landed and left for the US, but once the war started, it was discontinued. They used seaplanes at first, because of the heavy weight in fuel needed to cross the ocean; landing gear was not strong enough at that time to hold all the weight. Also, here was where Irish coffee was first served to passengers waiting to board. I suppose it would keep them relaxed for the flight.

Afterwards, we headed on into Limerick, and located our hostel we had found on the internet back at the library in Kilrush. We parked in the lot across the street from the dorm and unstrapping our gear from the bike, we carried all into the office. This was a dorm for a college of some sort during the winter, and in the summer it is rented out as a hostel. When a middle age man was checking us in, he was looking out at our bike and gear. Seeing we were from Minnesota, he asked us if our kids knew just what we were doing? When we explained we were also traveling by sailboat, maybe he thought he should call them to be sure we hadn't run away from home.

Limerick was fun to visit and we found interesting things to see, some restored buildings with grass roofs and of

157

course, antique shops. We took the bike uptown and parking was no problem, just shoehorn it in anywhere.

After we had returned to the marina, John, the manager had seen us on the way to Limerick and could only shake his head. I don't know, maybe we were the first crazy Americans he had seen touring Ireland this way. It was great.

I don't see how we could have experienced these things by flying in and renting a car for two weeks.

The summer ended, I found a building to park the motorcycle in and we stored away all the gear again for the winter, down in the boat. Next summer, we would sail up to Norway, and my plans were going to involve going to the Faeroe Islands before going to Norway. It would be tricky getting crew for that long of a trip.

2007 Kilrush to Norway

This coming season, will be more ambitious and it required a lot more planning. I had collected the necessary charts and sailing pilots for all the areas we planned to visit. Also, I had upgraded my navigation gear and made plans to revamp the water tanks and storage compartments. So the base plan would be for me to fly to Ireland alone early and work at getting the boat ready for sailing, while Marion and her friend Ronda, would fly over a few weeks later and tour Ireland. Then hopefully, like Marion would say, all the boat work would be done. She even wanted the bed made ready when she and Ronda were done touring. Ronda would fly back home. Marion and I would start off sailing by ourselves. Then we would meet up with Terry and two other boys, Ben and Michael Nelson. Ben had been along on the transatlantic trip in 2000. He proved to be an excellent crew, eager to learn sailing. His vouching for Michael, his younger brother, was good enough for me.

I got to Kilrush on May 15, and stayed at the hostel the first night, the boat being too full to lie down in as usual. It took a day to really get started on things. There was a ton of things to do before we could leave. To Marion's dismay, not all were done after their two week tour around Ireland. A list of the projects done before we actually left are as follows:

1. sanded, primed, undercoat and paint deck
2. sanded, primed and painted topsides
3. welded stainless steel rub bars for anchor rode
4. installed and plumbed electric bilge pump
5. chiseled out some protruding lead chunks in the bilge
6. installed new GPS and laptop programs
7. removed running lights to clean rust behind then, paint
8. did same to exhaust trim
9. installed rails or fiddles over shelves in cabin
10. removed forward ports to clean rust and paint
11. removed forward chocks, chipped and painted
12. cleaned rust from railings and painted
13. removed four cleats and welded on stainless ones
14. removed antenna bracket and welded on stainless one
15. fabricated stays'l boom

There was a lot of extra work that went along with these projects too. It all took time and when Marion arrived on the 16, we still had so much to do, so we didn't leave till the 28th of June.

Once launched, we motored over to the pontoons and kept putting things together. We had planned to leave later the next day, but Jan, a friend from last year, had studied the weather charts, and it looked like the time to go would be, early in the morning. We had to get locked out of the lagoon at high water and that was tonight. We would spend the night in the lock and leave early in the morning at low water. The lock wouldn't be open to the lagoon till later in the day tomorrow and the wind would be strong against us trying to motor out the 15 miles to the open ocean. We had to quickly fill our water jugs and get over to the lock fast, as it would be closing soon. We made it over in time and got locked in with the gate left open to the outside. There was still so much to do, lines and gear spread out across the deck and cockpit, a real mess. We worked till late at night or maybe early morning would be more accurate.

In the morning, the wind was light and the current was with us when we motored out. We had to get out to the open ocean before the current switched and the wind built up. As we neared the end of the Shannon River, we could feel the current slowing and the wind building against us. The water was getting very choppy and I could only hope the engine would not let us down now, it had been silent for two years.

When we broke out of the Shannon, and got in open water, I could raise some sail as we turned off the wind steering for the Aran Islands. I was so tired that I needed to rest. There had been too much activity in the past few days and little sleep. I trimmed the sails to park or lie hove-to. That way the boat would ride easily and slowly drift back to shore. Marion would stay awake and warn me if we got too close to shore, I took a cat nap.

When I woke, we had moved close to shore and it was time to move. We laid a course for the Aran Islands and sailed on. Early in the evening we arrived. It was a little tricky getting in from where we were coming from. It was high water, and it looked like we could sail in between two islands, but a check of the chart showed shallow water there, we took the long way around.

When we got to the anchorage, we were pleased to find visitor moorings saving us the trouble of anchoring. It was so nice to stop for a while and relax, to go to bed without worrying about the weather, or trying to get somewhere before dark, if we weren't going to stay out.

We had a good time at the island taking the tour to the fort. I got a chance to fix a jammed winch while there. While I was working on it, a lady from another boat came rowing over to talk. She and her husband had done some fantastic sailing, and I was impressed with all the places they had been.

We were still in good time to reach the boys and when we left the Aran Islands, we planned to spend the night out at sea heading for Blacksod Bay. The next day, we rounded the headland in some huge seas, not dangerous, but huge. I would think, with a foul wind it would be treacherous. As we sailed into the bay, it looked to be 10-miles long, we noticed a few buildings and some boats anchored, but we kept going and it got more desolate. We finally found a place to anchor in 20-feet of water.

That night, as low tide came in, I could feel the boat touch bottom. It was too late to move. In a few minutes we were solid aground. I sense immediately when the boat loses that buoyancy feeling, but Marion thought I was just crowding her side of the bed for no reason. Soon enough we were heeled over. Pots, pans, books and gear were falling to the floor. It was way too late to do anything. We had to wait for the tide to rise hopping the wind wouldn't pick up and flood us before we got upright. Luckily for us, the wind held off, and also it was dark, so our predicament didn't show from shore, I hoped.

As soon as we had water under us, we moved out to deeper water. I'm not sure why we lost 20-feet of water, as the tides are not that strong there, but maybe there is suction when the tide goes out that created it.

We anchored again in 30-feet of water, but now were more exposed to the weather. It came in one gale after another. We couldn't leave and we still had 300 miles to go to get the boys. Our meeting place was going to be a location in Scotland. We had to find a telephone and warn them that we would have to meet them here. We hoped they hadn't left the states yet.

In between gales, we picked up our anchor and 350-feet of anchor line and motored back to the beginning of the bay where we saw those boats. Maybe there would be a telephone there. We found a visitor mooring and surprise, a real phone booth. What luck! We managed to get a message to Ben and his brother before they left the states. Terry had already left; however, our daughter Mary was able to reach him via e-mail. Now we just had to wait. There was bus service to a larger town and we took it one day. This was good news, as the boys could use it to get over to us. Blacksod Bay was a very remote location.

Terry arrived on the 7ᵗʰ of July. He had got the e-mail while still in London and hadn't bought a ticket to Scotland yet. Now he needed to get a bus to the Irish Sea ferry, and another bus to Blacksod Bay, or actually a couple of buses. The last 20 miles, he would have to wait for a while, so he started walking, but was later picked up and driven to the boat. We knew when the bus was coming, so we had been out walking, and as we came to the dock prepared to wait for the bus, here comes Terry. It was a relief, so many things can go wrong and no communication makes it difficult to know what is happening.

The next day, we watched for the bus to come with the other two boys. I spied two forms standing on the dock with huge backpacks. Could that be them?

It was, and they had come prepared to do some camping on the way, a lot of gear to store away. Somehow we found a spot for everything, even though it was not handy to get to.

We were still getting one gale after another and couldn't leave yet. The wind was westerly and we would be close to a lee shore, not very safe. We waited.

On the 10ᵗʰ of July, it looked good enough to go and we started out. French Port, 15 miles up would be an anchorage for the night. The weather was a little windy, but allowed us to sail, and we made good time to French Port and our anchorage.

The next day, we left the anchorage and headed north. The wind was fair for us and sailing was good. The next stop would be in the Outer Hebrides. The first island would be Barra Island, about 200 miles away, where we can anchor in

Castle Bay. We had set up watches with Terry and Ben in one, and Michael and I in the other. Marion would be in charge of cooking, while the off watch would help her clean up.

One of the events that stick out in my mind with that leg happened the first night. Michael and I were on watch at 2:00 a.m., 75 miles north of Ireland and the sailing was pleasant. We could see stars above and no lights on the horizon. At sea, lights really stand out against the black background, so we felt in no danger from other craft. Suddenly, a ship's fog horn breaks the silence. Holy cow where was he? Quickly I jump down into the cabin and turn on the radar. It takes a few minutes to warm up, and soon I was searching out to 16 miles and closer. I couldn't find anything, but when I told Michael this, he said he heard the fog horn again. The ship had to be there, but where? Rechecking the radar, I found the ship only four miles out on collision course with us. We had ground fog that was blocking out his running lights, but lucky for us, he had us located on radar to warn of a possible collision. Quickly I had Michael change our course 30 degrees, to meet him on our starb'd side. I watched as our course and his started to separate on the radar screen. When he was directly abeam of us, one mile away on the radar screen, I looked out to see his ghostly shape slide by us.

The radar places a large drain on the battery when we aren't running the engine to provide electric power to the systems. So we hadn't been using it unless necessary, however, to be safe the rest of the night, we kept a close eye on the radar screen and would worry about charging the batteries later. The ground fog had fooled me into thinking we were safe since we could see no lights ahead, and with the stars overhead, we didn't think we were in the fog. With the rolling motion of the boat, the radar has a difficult time picking up ships, till they are very close, so we can't always rely on it either.

We had spotted the lighthouse flash about 25 miles away, and by morning we were sailing into Barra Island, the most southern inhabited island in the Outer Hebrides. The bay, called appropriately Castle Bay, was very scenic with the water, hills and a fully restored castle a little ways off the beach. There was a little village and a hostel located there, where for a charge, they would let us wash some clothes. One of the attractions of the Outer Hebrides is its remote location. People like to come here to avoid crowds I would guess.

A bus traveled around the island on a narrow black top road, so one day Marion and I packed a lunch and rode the bus to the south end of the black top. There we got out and walked over the hills to the beach. It was so interesting and easy walking as the sheep kept the grass down. A lot of interesting rocks to walk over, and at one point we could sit atop a hill and watch boats go through the pass. There was a lot of current, as we could see the boats crab into the current to maintain a straight course through the pass. We eventually came back to the road and waited for the bus to make his rounds. While we were waiting for the bus, we noticed a monument erected at the end of a bay. It was placed there to remember the great loss of lives aboard a ship that was blown into this bay during a storm.

The boys went exploring by themselves and traveled to the north end of the island.

The Hebrides are about 100 miles long, and with the light wind would take too long to sail. I decided that we would sail to the next island north, and take the bus all the way to the north end of the islands, to the town of Stornoway. The islands are close enough after Barra, so that by bridges and causeways and one ferry ride, you can ride the bus the whole length.

We left Barra early for Lockboisdale, the next island up. It was early enough in the day, so when we were close to the island in more shallow water, 50 feet I think, I tried fishing. Right away I pulled up five Mackerel on one line, a fish on every hook. It was pretty exciting for me as I seldom catch anything. I went on to haul in many more, it was fun. It has been the only time I can remember that I had enough fish to give away.

Here at Lockboisdale, we caught the bus and had a nice view of the islands as we traveled north. It was a long ride and the bus stopped along the way so the passengers could stretch. Stornoway was a fairly large city and we found a hostel to stay in. Ben and Michael decided to go out of town and camp, as they had brought along a tent and sleeping bags. We split up and wandered around the town to our own interests. I stopped at the local museum and while there used the restroom. I set down my newly bought movie camera, with all the picture chips from Marion and Ronda's trip in the camera bag as well. It wasn't till one half-hour later, I realized I had forgot the bag on the floor of the rest room. When I rushed back, it was gone. I felt terrible the rest of the day. Maybe some poor soul needed a camera and prayed for one, with fresh batteries too. He got his wish that day. Hope he enjoyed all our pictures we had on it too. It still hurts years later to think of it.

When we left Stornoway, minus my new camera, Ben and Michael were not on the bus. I was a little concerned, but they knew where the boat was, and they would find a way back I was sure. A few miles down the road, the bus stopped in the middle of nowhere and Ben and Michael climbed aboard. They had been camping on the top of a hill that night. Other than cold, it had been a good experience for them, great view in the morning when the sun came up. Scotland has what they call wild camping. You can camp out of town, and need permission if on private property, but there is much open land to camp on free with a great ocean view.

Back in Lockboisdale, we had noticed a bulletin advertising Highland games close by. We decided to take it in. We found a bus that would take us there, and it was an interesting day, watching the different types of games and dances.

Soon it was time to leave, and I had decided earlier, that due to lack of time, we would skip the Faeroe Islands and stop at Fair Isle instead. Marion and I had been at Fair Isle before, and it was an interesting and remote island. It was great for hiking and right on the way to Norway.

On the way to Fair Isle, we would make a stop at Westray, a north island of the Orkneys group. We had been there before on the way south from Norway in 2002. We could take the bus and ferry to another island to visit Kirkwall. The sail to Westray, was a mixture of weather and when we were about 10 miles off the west coast, the swells were getting a little rough. We were tacking and found it hard to come around. After a large wave knocked us over a bit, I decided to start the engine and pull us around. As soon as I put the transmission in gear, there was a loud thump and one of the halyards gave a jerk. What had happened was, when we got knocked over, one of the lines fell in the water. When the propeller started to turn, it began to wrap around the line. The line broke, but I didn't know if some of the line was still wound around the shaft. We still used the engine some, but once we got to the Pierowall Harbor in Westray, I would run up along the sea wall at high water and inspect the prop at low water.

We got into the harbor alright and the harbor master recognized us from before. I hope we had left a good impression last time. I remember that while there, we gave away a few items that we didn't use anymore. We were as glad to get rid of them, as I think they were to receive them.

As soon as we could, we motored up to the wall and tied her off. At low water, the prop and shaft looked OK, that was a relief.

We all took the bus to the ferry and then to Kirkwall, which must be the largest town in the group of islands. We had a good time poking around the town and by afternoon we made the return trip, ferry to bus.

When we left Westray, it was only a short hop to Fair Isle, but a check on the weather showed a nasty wind coming from easterly. I put it up to the crew to vote, whether they wanted to be holed up in Fair Isle for a few extra days or travel the 25 miles further to Lerwick and spend the time waiting there. There would be more to do in Lerwick, so they all voted to go to Lerwick. We waited out the foul wind there, and were glad to be off the ocean during this eastern blow.

After Lerwick, we had only one leg to go to Norway. Ben had made a phone call back to his parents in Minnesota to give them an ETA, but he wasn't sure it went through. They were coming to Norway, and would like to meet us on the coast and sail into Bergen with us.

When we came to the coast of Norway, we entered at the same place as in 2000. We tied up to the same dock. We were all very tired and after supper didn't stay up very late. The dock we were tied to had a large opening underneath and I was worried that at low water, we would slide partway underneath, creating a problem when the tide rose up. So in early morning, I got up as it was low tide, to check on the way the boat was lying to the dock. As soon as I slid the hatch back, a couple of people were standing on the dock looking at our boat. I first thought it was the owner of the dock, but it turned out to be Elden and Faith Nelson, the parents of Ben and Michael. They had flown in from Minnesota the night before, and gotten up early to take a bus out to the coast to find us. Thanks to some very helpful bus drivers, they were able to spot us. The bus dropped them off alongside the road to hike down to see if it was really us.

We fed them breakfast and coffee before heading the last 20 miles to Bergen. I'm afraid the jet lag caught up with them, and they had a good nap on the way in. We did get a chance to show them some sailing though. As a side comment, on the way in, Elden got a phone call from home saying the 35W Bridge in Minneapolis, had fallen in. We were all sorry to hear of this, as there were some lost lives and injuries too.

After arriving in Bergen, Ben and Michael left with their folks, and Terry traveled on to Copenhagen before flying home. Marion and I continued on with the boat to Norheimsund, making a stop first near Osoyro, where I had located a small bay to anchor in. We met some local folks traveling on a motorboat while there. The next day we made our regular stop in Uskadalen for the night, and later Norheimsund.

We parked the boat once more in Norheimsund, and after a short visit with Marion's relatives we flew home.

I had planned to sail next year to Sweden and the Baltic, but during the winter when I started to gather charts and guides, I felt the energy draining out of that idea, and started looking at the possibility of sailing back to the US instead. My original plan of building a boat and sailing back to our roots had been done and now it seemed I was just drifting around. As it turned out, it was the right thing to do, as I only had one more year of tough sailing in me. I would face a much more challenging battle in a couple of years and would not have been able to sail the boat back to the states.

2008 The Trip Back to America

I had chased down my dream of sailing back to our roots and much more. Maybe it was time to bring the boat back? That would be an adventure by itself. The more I thought about it, I was sure coming back would be the right thing to do.

I advertised in the local paper for anyone interested in making such a journey with me. I got a few calls, but none serious enough to consider. Taking Marion along was not even an option. Yes, she had proved able enough on the summer cruises, but on those trips we were always within a week, at the most, of making landfall. Also, she was limited in what she would be willing to do, and of course it's just plain dangerous at times, so that would add to my worries. Since she really never tried to learn much about sailing, I think she would become bored, and that would be hard on the rest of us. I would like to get people that would steer, plot a course, raise a sail, and cook, all while being short on sleep, wet and constantly tossed around. They would have to really want to go on the adventure. She wisely never considered going anyway.

I had posed the question to son, Terry and he agreed to come. He was working as a temp worker, but would tell his boss he would need the summer off. For that act of his, I'm forever grateful. Terry had sailed with me many times and knew the quirks of the boat, could sail the boat as well as I, and most important knew exactly what he was volunteering for. It would not be a vacation, since he was the only one going with me. That meant that we would be on watch four hours and off for four hours, 24 hours a day, week after week.

We arrived in Norway in early June, to find *Indian Summer* tied to the city dock waiting for us. It had been towed out to a marina close by for the winter, and on hearing that we were returning, the harbor master had brought our boat back to the quay. There was a pile of projects to get done before we could leave, and I had hoped that Terry would be a good helper. Marion needed to visit relatives and didn't have much time to help us get things ready.

All of the sailing gear had to be hauled up on deck and installed; sails, running rigging, cockpit lockers, always some painting, and also checking over all of the switches and fuses. Terry's bunk has a removable hatch over it, and it tends to leak, so he spent some time sealing it over to make it water tight. It paid off later when we were boarded by four different seas that would have soaked his sleeping bag and gear.

I had a port window in my bunk, that looked out to the cockpit area between the seats, and it was never water tight, but I never thought the cockpit would fill with water and soak my gear. I was wrong, and after the first soaking, always put my sleeping bag and clothes in a large garbage bag when they weren't being used to keep them dry. The salt air deteriorates everything on board whether it's being used or not.

We also found the throttle cable broken in one end, and in the other end, the throttle unit was rubbing on the frame of the boat. The first item I fixed by modifying a spare cable that I had along, but the other problem, required an exhausting time with the hacksaw, trying to remove a chunk of metal from the frame of the boat that was in the way of free movement for the throttle. Time was running out and I still had much to do. We had wanted to install a louder warning buzzer on the radar console, and it required a trip to Bergen to find the necessary plug to fit the outlet. Terry said he would go, and one of Marion's relatives would give him a ride to Bergen, since he travels there every day for work. Bergen is about 60 miles away, so Terry would take the bus back. He also found a 12-volt electric heater, that we thought would absorb some of the electric power the wind generator would develop, as my batteries are too small to take a large blast of current, making the generator idle a lot of the time when it could be shoving current in our batteries.

Terry came back and we were successful in installing

both items he brought back. I still had too much to do and hadn't bought any provisions yet, so I gave Terry money to go with Marion to buy two months' worth of groceries. Had I known how important food was to be on this trip, I should have taken the time to help pick out the food. They did the best they could, however, Terry eats a lot different than I. Marion is a much better cook than me, so a lot of the food didn't get used. One thing we did, when all the food was aboard, was to sort through the food to separate it in half. So we had equal amount of good stuff for the last half of the trip, not to be touched till the halfway mark. Also, adding to our stores was a bottle of Sailor Jerry Rum that Gerd's son-in-law thoughtfully gave us. Guess he thought the name fit us and we did enjoy celebrating any small milestone we achieved.

We left on time about 9:00 a.m., with Gerd and her two grandkids waving us off from the dock. We also saw her two daughters wave from their house and shop. Even my brother Steve and his wife Kelly were watching us from Minnesota, via the internet and the web cam at the marina, as we backed out of the slip. It was hard to believe we were off on the great voyage. Marion was along and would help steer on the way out of the fjord, about 60 miles. Two of her relatives, Kirsti and Mikjell Valland, would pick her up shortly before we got out on the ocean. She would stay in Norway for a few more days visiting before flying home.

We motored and sailed on our way out of the Hardanger Fjord. The wind was light and pleasant to be on the water. We stopped for the night at Uskadalen. It's a handy point between Bergen and Norheimsund, so we knew the place from past trips. We would leave Marion at a little town across the fjord from Uskadalen the next day.

We had a nice lunch on the dock next to the boat and

enjoyed our last evening together for a while. I know the voyage was on my mind and it was coming up fast. I guess if I was honest with myself, I would have given this trip back to the states second thoughts. As with every eve of my voyages, I felt no way to turn around, but go straight ahead as planned. So many problems could happen in the next two months and our skills as sailors and strength of the boat would surely be put to the test and many times. I know both Terry and I realize, that no matter how strong the boat, or how experienced the sailor, there are situations at sea that cannot be survived. We needed the sea to let us pass though. We had planned as much as we could; now we would see if it was enough.

The next morning was bright and calm, and Marion steered us out of the harbor while Terry and I cleaned up the dock lines and fenders, getting the boat ready for traveling. It didn't take long to get across the fjord to the pickup place on the island of Tysnesoy, where Marion's relatives would pick her up.

There was some confusion as to just where the town was, so we motored along the shore looking with binoculars for a place to tie up. We found a nice spot, and after tying up and stepping ashore, we saw the keep off sign. Around the corner, we did see some boats tied to a small pontoon, so we thought that is where we should be. So untying, we motored over and were just about to come to the dock, when the owner came out hollering for us not to be there. Seems that it is too shallow for us and we could snag his holding cables. He said the first place we were at was OK for a while, so back we went. He was friendly (we never did meet a crabby Norwegian) and stayed and talked for a while till Marion's relatives came. He was a retired merchant marine sailor and had crossed the Atlantic about fifty times, but never in anything as small as our boat. He just laughed at our planned voyage. After a couple of pictures and a good hug from Marion, and good byes said to Kirsti and Mikjell, we cast loose the lines and backed away. It was kind of sad, so I was glad to be away and focus on the trip ahead. There was work to do now.

We spent the rest of the day working our way toward the North Sea, and shortly before the exit we came to a nice protected bay. It was just perfect for a good night's rest. It was perfectly still and so quiet in there. Across the bay or lagoon were a few houses and boats, but nothing stirring. Looking on shore, close to the boat, was a picnic table, and I suppose, if it weren't so much trouble to put the skiff together, we would have rowed ashore and gone for a walk.

Next morning was overcast and hard to tell the direction of the wind from our protected anchorage. We motored out and were tempted to take a short cut through some small islands, but decided to play it safe and go all the way around. Soon we were in the open ocean and the wind was fair, we shut off the engine and set the auto-pilot. This was sailing, as good as it gets. The wind was fair all the way across the North Sea, so we made good time, one hundred miles in twenty-four hours not fast, but comfortable. So two days later, about six in the evening, we came to Fair Isle. It was raining and the entrance to the harbor was tricky, so we lay hove-to the rest of the night. We were on four-hour watches, so one of us was awake all the time. In the morning, we had drifted a short distance away from the island, but we still had it in sight. We sailed in, following the directions of keeping the sheep's head just in line with the breakwater outer rocks.

I think there was only the ferry from Lerwick and a Norwegian sailboat there. Later an English sailboat came and rafted up to us. The toilet had plugged and we had that to fix while the boat was lying calm. We had just missed a big sheep round-up, that would have been fun to take part in, but we hiked around the island, one end to the other anyway. We met a few people while on our hikes. A couple were there as volunteers to help the residents with their chores, and another lady who was about to leave after working on the island for a while. The hiking was very nice, as the sheep kept the grass down to golf course level, and a lot of interesting rocks, gullies and cliffs to explore. There were a couple of roads on the island that we walked on from one end to another. Later, another boat joined us, an English training boat and they rafted up to us. It is common courtesy when leaving your boat to go ashore, that you always walk across your neighbors boat forward of the mast. That is so the owners have privacy, since most of the time the main hatch is left open. It was an obstacle course for the English boat people to do, so we told them they could cross over in our cockpit, in full view of our cabin.

One day, we were lighting our diesel fueled stove, and it is a bugger to get lit. We always used red spirits to start it, and it always gave off a 12-inch flame first. Just as we had lit the fuel and the flame did its thing above the stove, the captain of the English boat walked across ours and saw the flame. He made a startling comment, but we assured him all was well and normal. At any rate they left the next day, maybe to get out of harm's way.

Just before our departure, I was cleaning up and decided to pump out the bilge. I hadn't realized that there was a very small leak in the fuel line to the engine, and it had run down to the bilge. Well, after pumping out the water, our boat had sheen all around in the water, next to the hull. Terry hit the ceiling when he saw this. I suppose if he had a choice he would have left me and the boat there. He didn't, thank God, and we cast off the lines and headed for the Orkneys.

We caught the current just right, thanks to some good local knowledge, and made Pierowall in the Orkneys by late afternoon. I was just planning to anchor near the harbor and wait out the next favorable current, but outside the harbor was a visitor mooring. It made tying up so easy. We had put the skiff away, back in Norway, so we just stayed on the boat for a good rest. When the current turned in our favor, we just dropped the mooring line and were off.

Our next stop would be Stornoway in the Outer Hebrides. We bypassed some tidal rips on the north side of the island. With the binoculars we could see a lot of confused water and were glad not to be a part of it. Thanks in part for good charts of the area. As we approached Cape Wrath, on the north coast of Scotland, the wind died and I got out my fishing rod. I had yet to catch any fish and didn't want to stop the boat to fish. While we were waiting for wind, this would be a good chance. I no sooner got settled in and the wind came back. It was time to sail.

We pushed on, and by evening the fog had rolled in. We turned on the radar and kept plotting our position on the chart. I didn't have a chart plotter then, and had to keep reading our latitude and longitude from the GPS, and locating our position on the chart. The radar would show us any vessels on collision course with us. We slowly made our way into the harbor. When we were close, Terry made a call to the harbor master for a place to tie up. He responded with directions and said he would be available to take our lines.

We arrived at low tide and found the dock was ten-to twelve-feet above us.

It was so nice to be tied up again. I don't seem to get too anxious when out to sea, but when coming into shore, there are a host of dangers to deal with, and fog, and a strange harbor doesn't help matters.

Here in Stornoway; we could check e-mail, see if Marion was getting our Spot Check,(updates on our position), take showers at the public bathroom downtown, top off our diesel and water, and finish up grocery shopping. Terry had informed me that he would eat nothing with wheat in it, so we had to buy more food he would eat.

As we passed by the liquor department, we studied it closely and thought maybe a small bottle of rum, trawler rum to be exact, might be needed on certain occasions. Like when we reached the halfway point. Alas, the small bottle of rum was needed for so many small celebrations, that by the time halfway was reached the strongest thing we had to drink was coffee.

Marion had started getting our positions after a few days, the problem being, that Terry didn't know the importance of laying the transmitter right side up, and I had neglected to tell him this important piece of information.

In Stornoway, we got our exit papers to show US customs when we arrived there, a small fact I had overlooked. We also removed our poor sails for the best ones I had. Then we took the anchor and all the anchor chain off the bow and stowed it under the floorboards. This would give the bow more buoyancy when meeting large waves. We did the same thing with the outboard motor that normally rides on the stern rail. I saw that the main hatch that I made out of oak wood many years ago was falling apart in places. So I put extra screws in it.

While we were in Stornoway, a search was out for an overdue sailboat from the states that highlighted the dangers of our trip. We met a couple of US boats while there, and it was strange enough to have three US boats there at the same time, that local people came down to see us.

Just before leaving, a boat had come in and rafted up to us. He was afraid to let his lines go and circle around to let us out. He wanted to pass his dock lines over us as we motored out. I didn't like this idea, because of our wind vane steering being in a position to get caught in the lines and damaged. It went OK, with only a few anxious moments for us, but we got away without damage. The current, we saw, was making a lot of problems for the other boat and we were sure glad to be out of the mess.

We had to motor sail into the wind for a while, to get around the top of the island, just like at the Orkneys. As we plowed our way north, dolphins swam along and in front of us giving us a good send off. The wind was northeast and was a fair wind for us. When we rounded the top corner of the Hebrides, we could shut off the engine, put up more sail, and set the autopilot.

Our first goal was to get to 50 degrees latitude and 40 degrees longitude. This would give us a chance to take advantage of any low pressure systems passing below us and give us an east-blowing wind. However, much of the time we had wind close to our path, and had to sail north or south of our desired course. My boat will only sail about 55 or 60 degrees to either side of the wind, and if the wind is strong, not even that. Some days, we just trimmed the sails to kind of keep the boat headed into the waves and slowly get pushed backwards.

On July 12, the wind had left us, so I got out the fishing rod and in no time caught three eating size fish. Terry wasn't interested in eating fish, so I had them all to myself. I filleted them and added them to boiling potatoes, delicious. We smelled sea-weed even though we were hundreds of miles from land; we surmised that the smell was coming from Rockall Bank. Rockall Bank is a shallow area with a 60-foot rock sticking out of the water, about 200 miles from Ireland. It's a good area to avoid.

On July 14, we were sailing with double reef main and staysail, our heavy weather set-up. Conditions were rough. By July 15, the wind had headed us, so it was no use to keep sailing. We deployed the sea anchor. It is a 15-foot wide parachute attached to 400-feet of anchor line, tied off at the bow. The idea is that the chute would keep the boat from drifting backwards too fast. It helped. We were both so tired from all the work getting it ready, and also from our four on and four off watches. I declared a holiday and said we could both rest, no one on watch. We were in such a lonely part of the ocean and visibility was good. It was the middle of the day; I felt that we could rest safely. I believe we stayed there a day and a half and lost about 10 miles.

After we got all the line pulled in and the sea anchor aboard, we raised a small head sail and double reefed the main sail. By back-winding the head sail i.e., pulling the sheet line from the sail on the opposite side that we would normally use while sailing, that keeps the boat from sailing across the wind and also keeps the boat from moving forward, essentially parking the boat. It positions the boat more head on to the waves making it easier to ride out bad weather. Since the wind had not yet come fair for us, we still had to wait it out. At least we were ready.

On July 17, we had the sails trimmed and moving again. It was depressing to sail up though our drifting track. The GPS drops small dots every so often, like bread crumbs from the Hansel and Gretel story, and these were what we sailed back through. At three knots, it would take over three hours to get back to the start point where we started drifting.

Sometime later, it's not recorded in my log surprisingly, the wind had died and as we lay becalmed, I started fishing again. Terry was sleeping below as it was my watch. As I lay on the deck, rocking to and fro, enjoying the peaceful scenery, the jib came crashing down. I jumped up, and when I looked at the halyard, the line that hoists up the sail, I saw it was worn through. Evidently during the night, while changing sails, the line had got rapped around the forestay, and when the sail was hoisted to the top, chaffed on the line till it parted, letting the whole halyard drop down inside the mast, 50 feet down. I saw right away, that someone needed to get to the top of the mast, and drop down a messenger line, down inside the mast, to be attached to the broken line and hoist it up again.

On waking Terry, he wasn't too keen on doing anything as dangerous as pulling me up to the top of the mast, but I wouldn't think of giving this job, of going to the top, to anyone else. I was anxious to get it done before any wind came up. As it was, the top of the mast was swaying back and forth maybe three feet with just the swells. I had a small canvas swing chair that can be attached to any of the remaining halyards, and by using the winch, be cranked up to the top. All went fine. Terry practiced pulling me up a ways and lowering me down before the real thing.

When I got to the top, I needed both hands to thread in the line, and had to push myself around to the front of the mast, and hold myself there with my knees. I didn't dare let go, for fear of swinging away from the mast and then come swinging back into the mast. It took maybe 20 minutes at the top to get the messenger line down to Terry, where he had to tape it on the end of the halyard and start threading it through the mast again. By the time I got down, my knees were shaking from the strain of holding on to the mast, but we felt so good about getting the line up again. The boat just won't sail with just the main, and we had a long way to go yet.

On July 20, I made contact with a ham operator from Finland, named Jurgen. He was German, but spent summers in Finland. He was most helpful, and contacted Marion by e-mail to let her know we were OK. I did give him our latitude and longitude, but since we send daily reports via Spot she should know our position. My antennas were poor on the boat, but I did manage to get through a few more times. When we were closer to Newfoundland, I was able to contact a fellow in Florida, that put in a phone patch to Marion for me also.

On July 27, Terry computes our progress and miles to go, and thinks that if we maintain our current rate, we should reach Maine on September 9. Also, he has been checking our fresh water, and if we continue at the current rate, we will be dry on August 27. We decide to watch water usage and collect any rain water that comes our way. It has been remarkably dry most of the way, but as we close in on the Grand Banks, we get misty rain with the fog. Fog can come in anytime, and we are glad to have radar available. We practice picking out ships the few times we see them and try to get used to its capabilities.

When we reach the Grand Banks, we are slowly sailing westerly, and haven't seen any ships for weeks, and only the wind and water sounds have been heard. Terry is below and I'm standing on deck, when I hear a motor. Looking around I finally see an airplane flying low and coming straight for us. Right before he reaches us he pulls up and we see it's the Canadian Coast Guard. I think they were out looking for icebergs and decided to look us over. Then later, we see a fishing trawler with a Coast Guard cutter standing by. We hear on the radio that they will send over an inspector to look over their catch. The Coast Guard launches a rib boat and after dropping off the inspector, they come over to us to chat. We had no fish for them to inspect, the last fish caught was those three, about a month ago.

As we made our way west through the Banks, we started to get more rain. As a precaution, we started to collect rain water. When it looked like we would get a steady rain, I dropped the main sail down about a foot or so. This created a fold in the lower part of the sail. After a few minutes of rain, I would taste the water collected in the fold. If it didn't taste salty or have a sail canvas taste to it, I would bucket it in a fresh water container.

We turned south to stay on the outside of Sable Island, before turning west again for Maine. Sable Island has a bad reputation of wrecking ships, due to the strong currents, shallow water, shifting sandbanks, and fog. We had no trouble staying away from it with our good GPS position, anytime we wanted. As we came closer to the tip of Nova Scotia, the wind started to build.

We were 65-miles east of the tip of Nova Scotia or half way between Sable Island and the mainland. Everything is wet with sea water and had been for weeks. I think we must have smelled like some old billy goats. We couldn't think of anything more enjoyable than a hot shower in fresh water and clean clothes.

But now, the wind had been increasing throughout the day from a good direction for us. We had been running down our course with only the main sail let out most of the time, and we were reeling off the miles. My watch had started four hours ago, and two hours ago, I woke Terry up to shorten sail. *Indian Summer* was letting me know we were pushing too hard by shipping a lot of water over the rail, and bad things happen when gear breaks in a rough sea.

Later, when Terry came on deck to begin his four-hour watch, the waves were huge, close to 20-footers, but the boat was riding them well. We had the smallest sail up, and we were still traveling at the boat's maximum speed. By midnight, I could tell we had to slow her down some more. The waves were even more impressive. Huge walls of water would rise up from the stern and then break with long, white water running down the face of the wave. Anything higher than our 31-inch free board would flow freely across the deck. With Terry steering the boat, keeping the stern into the waves, I crawled to the foredeck and managed to claw down the small staysail. I had a much smaller storm sail to put up, however, I had never used it on this boat before, and of course it didn't fit. It took some jury-rigging to make it work well, all under rather bouncy conditions, in the dark, with water streaming across the deck.

An hour later, I had the smaller sail jury-rigged and working for us. It wasn't a pretty sight, but with all that wind, it didn't take much to move the boat along. Our speed was cut in half, and the boat and crew were happy. The wind approached gale-force strength for the rest of the night, but we had the appropriate sail up for it and rode through it in fine style. With those kinds of waves, it's important to keep moving and have some speed on, to steer around bad conditions. By noon the next day, the wind decreased in strength, and we had all sails set again. We felt good that we had passed the test and came out with no gear or crew damaged, and our confidence soared.

On August 17, we were sailing merrily across the Bay of Maine, with hardly any waves and at our cruising speed. We had figured out a way around the islands to get to Billing's Marina at Stonington and soon we were tied up at the fuel dock.

I had focused so much on the trip across the ocean I had neglected to read up on proper entry into the states. A few years ago, we had sailed to Cuba and on returning we had just called customs to report in. They had come down to see us, but that was how it was done then. Well, now things were different after 9/11, and customs were not too happy how we came in. There are only certain points of entry, and Stonington wasn't one of them. We were to report to Belfast the next day, and see what kind of trouble we were in. Belfast is one and a half-hour drive away and we had no way of getting there. Luckily for us, we knew a brother of a neighbor of ours lived in Stonington, and after calling him to see if he had any ideas, he said we could use a spare car of theirs for the day. What a lucky break.

We reported as instructed, and after a good tongue lashing and information on how things should have been done, we were off the hook. However, we were told in no uncertain terms, that this free pass would only work this time, next time it would be different.

The next few days, were spent putting the boat away for the winter. Terry's girlfriend drove over from Minneapolis to pick him up and also gave me a ride to the airport in Bangor. They spent the next few days driving back to Minnesota and I flew home at warp speed. After traveling weeks at anywhere from one-to six-miles an hour, the jet was traveling over 500 hundred miles an hour.

So ends the adventure started back in 1986. I don't know if I'll ever get a chance to do something like that again, because the next year I was diagnosed with cancer and a whole different battle began.

2012 Maine to Nantucket and Martha's Vineyard

In 2009, I became ill with cancer, so went through a transplant and recovery that took years. In 2011, Marion and I made a trip out to the boat to do a little maintenance, i.e., sand and paint the peeling deck. I knew I wasn't strong enough to make a sailing trip yet, but I was hoping by next year I would be up to it.

During the winter of 2011-2012, I was able to line up crew for the trip to Nantucket and return. Our son Terry would join Marion and I for the off-shore run down to Nantucket, about a three-day sail. He could be away from his job with Medtronics for two weeks. He would stay with us while we visited Nantucket, and then we would sail over to Martha's Vineyard, where he could catch a ferry to the mainland, a bus to Boston, and train to Minneapolis. Planes are faster, but flying isn't much fun anymore, and he wanted to see some points of interest on the way out.

After Terry would leave, Marion and I would run the boat for the next three weeks, sailing west through Woods Hole gap and over to the mainland, anchor for a while then sail up through the Cape Cod Canal and north to

Provincetown. We would anchor there and wait for son-in-law Bruce Droogsma and his dad, Chuck, to fly into Boston from Minneapolis. Then they would take the ferry from Logan Airport in Boston out to Provincetown, a distance about thirty-five miles. A friend of ours, Ned McDonnell, who works on the ferry, arranged tickets for them. The four of us would then sail north to Stonington, Maine, where we had left our car with friends. Marion would get off the boat there and take the car farther north to a different marina, where I had previously arranged to winter the boat, while the three of us would sail the boat to the new marina.

It was a complicated sailing plan, with many plane and train and bus schedules to meet. The crew had already purchased their tickets well in advance of the trip, with no refund available, so I was under some pressure to see that they got beached on time. Marion and I would be driving home, and so, we had no time constraints. Of course there was the little matter of *Indian Summer*, which had been sitting idle for four years after making a difficult trans-Atlantic voyage. Who knows what systems had been compromised? In 2008, we did have a few equipment failures on the way home that were jury-rigged, and they had to be sorted out too. Also, my doctor didn't like the idea of me missing a regular check-up appointment, so I had to figure out a way of squeezing in a doctor visit back in Minnesota sometime in June. There would be plenty of opportunity for things to go wrong.

I knew three major items had to be worked on. First, was the rotting main hatch needed to be replaced, I had taken measurements earlier and wanted to make this one from aluminum. Second, was some serious rusting in the cockpit around the drain hole, it needed a new plating welded in.

Third, were the topsides. The previous year, Marion and I had done the deck, but the sides where badly peeling also. Those were the known projects. Who knows what other problems had developed over the past four years? All boaters know, boats deteriorate a little each day and it makes no difference if they are being used or not.

A friend of mine, John Carstens, had expressed an interest in coming out to help me ready the boat for the season. He didn't care to go sailing though. He is a retired engineer and very handy with tools. He has built and paddled many canoes, built and remodeled many homes, and a host of other fine accomplishments. Also, being six-foot-seven he could get by without using a stepladder while we painted the boat. I on the other hand, top out at five-foot-one, handy for those low places. I remembered another friend who so graciously volunteered to come to New Orleans and help get the boat ready for the transatlantic voyage in 2000, Steve Reynolds. It's so nice to have friends like that. John did follow through with his desire to come, and he was a terrific help to me.

There was much planning in the early months of 2012. I had charts to study and boat projects to plan beyond the big three, gather all the necessary tools and equipment needed, plus find a vehicle to haul all this stuff out to Maine. I had quit driving a 1994 Toyota a few years ago, and it had been just sitting in the grass across from my shop. I wondered if there was still life left in it, so I bought a new battery and after installing it, the engine ran beautifully. The 220,000 miles on the odometer, made me wonder when it would quit, but I would give it a chance. I lined up my April doctor appointment to coincide with my drive to Maine, as it was on the way, four hundred miles south of home.

My doctor appointment was April 24, and immediately after the visit, headed for Maine with a stop in Yorkville, Illinois, to meet up with John, who drove separately having stopped off at Milwaukee to visit a friend. We spent the night at my brother-in-law's place. His wife, Eileen fixed us a good supper and breakfast before we left. We drove pretty steady, staying in communication with our cell phones. Sometimes we got separated, but it was easy to link up again after a phone call. We came to Boston, where John and his wife Sue have a daughter. We spent the night there and then turned north to Maine. We arrived in Stonington, and the boat on Saturday. We unpacked the vehicles, found a ladder to get into the boat and made plans for work to start Sunday.

Where the boat was parked, we had no electrical power, so we ran a cord across the road to a working outlet. We started in on the top-sides first, since painting would be dependent of the weather, and the weather then was nice. John handled all the sanding from the ground, using some scaffolding he had brought along. I worked along the top of the rail crawling in and out of the standing rigging and reaching down as far as I could.

By Monday, we had one side done and starting on the other side. By now, the shipyard workers had returned to work from the weekend, and John went to look for the yard foreman, Don, to see about electric power for us. We didn't like to have our power cord driven over so often, now that there was so much vehicle activity. Don was surprised that we would need electric power, and when John told him we were sanding the top sides, he said that was forbidden in this yard, only his workers could do that work, from the rail on down. Well, John told him that Jerry had said it was OK to work above the waterline.

"Who is Jerry," he asked defiantly?

"Well, he owns this boat and he said that is what the yard told him three years ago, when he first came here."

"Well, he is wrong, but since you have already started, you can finish."

We did finally get some closer power and got on with the projects. I didn't get any "Good Mornings," from Don the rest of our stay there.

I enjoy living on the boat, even if it's in dry dock, so I always planned on working, eating and sleeping right on the boat. The boat cabin was not made for crew much over six-feet-tall, so John couldn't spend much time in the cabin. Also, he had his dog, Ketcher, along and he was not the ladder climbing type, so John preferred to set up cooking facilities on the ground. He had brought along a bed in his van, along with most of his shop tools, scaffolding and wood supplies. It did take an engineer to pack all that stuff and still have room for a driver and his dog. A couple of days into the project, I guess the yard hadn't seen this type of setup before, and we were getting hints that we were looking a little too permanent. So we kind of cleaned up our job site, made it look like we were just there for the weekend. We stayed five weeks.

We were making such good progress on the boat, that on the rainy days, we went into town to eat breakfast or sometimes supper. The Harbor Café was highly recommended and it was a treat to eat out. Of the three main projects, painting top-sides, main hatch replacement and steel plates welded in the cockpit, we concentrated on the painting whenever the weather was good. The others could be done in less sunny days of which there were plenty, it was Maine you know.

We did get the sides painted in between rain showers and started work on the new main hatch. My brother, Steve, was kind enough to locate some aluminum and bend the corners for me. John and I assembled it with aircraft rivets at the boat. It was a good fit and now strong enough to stand on while reefing the main sail. I also would feel much better the next time a boarding sea rushes over the boat. I had brought along a 110-volt welder for the last big project, welding in replacement plates in the aft end of the cockpit. Sea water has a tendency to collect there, and not able to get to the drain hole, so it's a good place to start rusting. It was a curved piece that required some special forming to make it fit properly. We primed and painted all, and it turned out very well. We did have a few switches and a solenoid to replace, along with some more painting on the deck, and run up the running rigging.

This last item proved to be a little challenge for us. When I leave the boat for the year, I like to replace the running rigging with smaller line to keep the rigging from UV damage from the sun. I do this by taping the small line to the larger line and pulling up the outside of the mast and down the inside. Well, you can imagine our horror to feel the two lines part while making the turn at the top of the mast, fifty feet up. Now, we had the entire jib halyard on the deck with no small line to hoist it up to the top of the mast. It had happened once before on our return trip across the Atlantic, due to a chaffed line and I knew what had to be done. John would have to hoist me by the winch to the top of the mast, so I could send down the messenger line for him to grab at the bottom. I'm not afraid of heights, only falling from them, plus my back was still in recovery, so not a good place to throw your back out. John had a little misgiving about this

191

whole business, since he was not used to cranking and slipping a winch. We did a few practice runs close to the deck before going to the top. Things went fairly smooth, and a little while later, we had all four halyards hoisted to the top and around their pulleys. If we were drinking men, it would have called for a shot of something strong to celebrate, but instead we just said, "Glad that's over with!"

There were some raining cool days that we couldn't get much done, so we did some exploring around. I was looking for a different marina to winter my boat at, and John was looking for a replacement phone, his had packed up and he was out of touch with his family. We drove many miles in search of these two things, and even with two GPS units and a map, got totally lost. The fog didn't help us much either. Maine's coastline is a little confusing, going from point A to point B. We found that at times we were on the wrong side of the bay.

By the 18th of May, it was time to leave Stonington and drive to Boston. We would stay at Anna and Blake's apartment till the 22, when I would fly back to Minnesota for another doctor appointment. John would drive back to Minnesota alone, no convoy this time. I had decided to go all the way back to Wannaska for a few days, and fix whatever had broken while I was gone. The riding lawnmower had caught fire and needed some rework Marion said, and I would be surprised if that was all to fix. I always have this feeling that everything is falling in behind me, as I drive away from home.

I was home in Wannaska for about a week, before Marion and I left for my doctor appointment at Mayo Clinic in Rochester, Minnesota. It was on the fourth of June, and we flew out of Minneapolis on the sixth. We arrived in

Boston that day and picked up our car at Anna's and drove to Stonington, with a stop in Winterport, Maine, to give the new marina owners, a time when I would return with my boat and end our summer cruise.

As much as I like sleeping on the boat, it's not Marion's cup of tea. Since Wendy and Bill had so graciously offered their place for us to stay, while we put the finishing touches to the boat, we spent our evenings with them enjoying a good supper and a comfortable bed to sleep in. Marion loved it and I guess a little comfort couldn't hurt. There would be plenty of discomfort when we got offshore, and I would need a few points in my column then.

It took Marion and me a week to finish getting the boat ready. As if I didn't have enough to worry about, I had chipped a tooth a few days earlier and didn't know if I should try to get it fixed on such short notice, or take a chance that it wouldn't bother me all summer. Wendy just happens to own the local dentist office and luckily for me, there was a cancellation in time to fit me in. Of course it wasn't just a simple chipped tooth, because when she started to work on it more fell off, but Wendy got it fixed up just fine anyway. Things were going smoothly; we were organizing all the stuff that we had piled in the boat from the last trip. There was a little more room now, after we had removed unused gear last year, and hauled it home in the trailer.

When the marina set us in, I don't think the crane operator thought the engine would even start, because I heard him say, "That's amazing," when the engine started right up. He knew it had been four years since we sailed in, and my boat was becoming a permanent fixture there I think. I wish I could blame someone else for this following mistake, but I was the one who put the fuel selector in the wrong position, pumping fuel into a full tank. Before we got to the pontoon, we had left fuel sheen behind us from fuel running overboard. I don't suppose we could have lost even one half-gallon but it looked bad. I quickly bought a bunch of pads at the boat store that soak up fuel not water and we spent a few hours cleaning up the mess. After that incident, we got back to last minute preparations that had to be done before leaving.

The last night we stayed at Bill and Wendy's they cooked up lobster and that was a treat. Bill is a man of many skills and one was lobster fisherman. He has moved on to other things now, but he knows lobsters inside and out. He walked us two rookies, through the cracking and eating of a lobster, explaining each type of meat found on the animal. It's more complicated than white or dark meat on a turkey.

The next night, we spent on the boat and I was anxious to get away, but we had to wait for high tide to get clear of the shallows in the marina. Marion and I left the marina about 9:30, on the 18th of June. Sailing south out the Deer Island Thorofare, zigzagging around lobster pot buoys, we turned westward up the Penobscot Bay, to a small island that looked like a good spot to anchor from the chart. Hog Island had a small bay or cove with twenty feet of water, a good depth for us to set the hook down.

We arrived late in the afternoon, and found just the spot we had hoped for. It was so nice to be afloat again. It had been almost four years since I was able to be a sailor again. I enjoy the challenge of planning and carrying out a voyage. This spot was so peaceful, we stayed an extra day, just putting the boat right again. It was time to get on "boat time" in other words, slow down. When a boat is ashore for so long, things are not put in their proper place, and it takes some time to find the right home for everything. Some things have to be close at hand and others, that are not used very often, stored farther away. It takes time to figure it all out.

After the second day, we pulled anchor and motored across the bay, no wind, to the city of Belfast on the 21st of June. We would hang out there till Terry would arrive on the bus, having taken the train to Portsmouth. I inflated our rubber raft and placed the ten-horse Johnson on behind. We were ready to go ashore. I did notice that the cooling water coming from the Johnson was very slow and getting hot, so the maintenance troubles were starting. We made it to the city dock OK, and it felt strange to be walking anywhere again, our legs were a little stiff. We checked out the library for e-mail, got a prescription filled at the pharmacy and visited a few stores to get some supplies. When walking, especially in a hilly town like Belfast, it gets tiring fast, so we kind of hung out close to the waterfront. Later that day we returned to the boat and it was nice to be back home again, with everything we need right here in the boat.

Saturday, we sent a text to Terry, to see where he was and what time he would arrive. We went in about noon and drifted around till he came. He had to hike about one mile from the bus station to the water. I like the way he travels, light. A small backpack and duffel bag, that's good enough for two weeks. On a small boat there is very limited space for stuff, the boat gear taking up most of the lockers, so it can be a problem if one is a heavy packer.

We were all anxious to get underway again, so we left the next morning, sailing down the bay to our next port of call, Rockland. We had light winds during the day and sailed slowly southerly, about four in the afternoon, we pulled in the sails and started to motor in, wanting to get the hook down before dark. Rounding the breakwater we came to a large anchorage, and selected a spot on the chart where the depth was only around twenty-feet. There was a windjammer already anchored there and was a little too noisy. It must have been happy-hour for the passengers, so we decided to move on, that's when the idling engine quit. When a diesel engine stops it normally means out of fuel, since there is no ignition parts to a diesel. We of course just set the anchor right there, kind of like setting the parking brake, as we didn't want to drift into thinner water than we already had. Tides are around ten-feet here. Well, I hadn't changed the fuel-filter yet this year, so I thought maybe it was just plugged. I always carry lots of spare parts with, so I proceeded to replace the filter, after which the engine restarted, no problem I thought.

We launched the rubber raft and went ashore, soon it began to rain. The city dock had a charge of five dollars per skiff parking fee. We made the short hike into town and poked around some stores. I walked with Marion to the library, so she could check up on any e-mail. I left her there and found a marine store, where I bought a folding ladder to help Marion get from the raft to the boat; the old one had developed some serious cracks that Terry had noticed. After the marine store, I just wandered around kind of waiting for the time we were to meet at a convenience store, near the dock, when I found Terry wandering around too, looking for a place to get a beer. I walked with him to a café, where he found his beer and I got coffee. I think we both feel towns are a bit overrated. Seems like it's a destination we work to get to, but after we're there, we wonder, "What for?" We did pick up a few groceries and some ice though.

We met Marion at a Walgreen's Store that had a good selection of groceries and other items we needed, so we stocked up and hiked back to the dock. Of course it started to rain in earnest on the ride back to the boat, so we were all super soaked by the time we reached the boat. After changing clothes, we had a warm supper by candlelight and turned in, we were to leave tomorrow for the next port, Tenants Harbor.

There was fog in the morning, but decided to leave anyway. We plotted a course outside of a group of islands and hoped things would clear up as we went. It didn't, and we had fog most of the day dodging lobster pots as we went. Later in the afternoon, we entered Tenants Harbor, and turned into Long Cove, a recommended anchorage. Before we had made the turn, the engine quit. We got it started right away, but it kept stopping on us. We limped over to the side of the fairway and anchored. It has to be a fuel problem, I was sure, so maybe the fuel tank needed a good cleaning. The forward tank is the easiest to get to and after removing the cleanout cover, we saw a lot of dirty fuel. So this was my problem I thought, dirty fuel plugging the filters. Terry and I mopped up the remaining fuel and gave the tank a good cleaning. We poured in clean fuel and once again changed the fuel filter. Now I restarted the engine and let it run for one hour. It surely must be fixed right this time, I thought. We decided to relax the rest of the day and get a fresh start in the morning. We would be heading offshore for Nantucket, about a three day run, against prevailing winds from the south, our new course.

We got underway as planned the next day, motoring out through the lobster pots again. The wind was light, so we kept the engine going. About one hour out, while motoring at half throttle, the engine just quit. I was starting to run out of ideas now. I told Terry to help get the sails up, we would

197

continue on our course while I thought about diesel engines and what makes them stop.

We sailed on through the day and rest of the night. By the next day, I had decided that the mechanical fuel pump must be at fault. I had carried an electric fuel pump as a spare part in case this problem came up. The electric pump would fit right in the fuel line between the filter and the mechanical pump. Luckily, the pump came with fittings that would fit my existing fuel line. In a couple of hours I was ready to try it out. The engine started up fine and continued to run. We would have to see how it worked while under way for a while. The engine was important for getting us into port and anchor, but also for keeping the batteries charged up. I had quit using the wind generator, as it was too noisy and took so long to charge up my batteries.

We were well offshore by now, and dealing with southerly wind, requiring us to tack back and forth, traveling a much farther distance than the original 200 miles to Nantucket. Terry and I were switching off every three hours, while Marion took care of things in the cabin. Sailing down the outside of Cape Cod the third night, we arrived at the entrance to Nantucket Sound, early in the morning. There were tide issues to consider now. There can be a two knot current running with or against us, and since we only make five knots under power, or four to five knots under sail normally, we had to get all the help we could from the current flow. The current was in our favor about seven that morning, so we started into the sound, 27-miles to go or about five more hours to Nantucket. There was light wind, so we had a chance to try out the new electric fuel pump. It didn't miss a beat all the way in.

Entering the harbor was easy, even though it was very

busy with boats of all sizes coming and going. We first cruised through the mooring field looking for other anchored boats. I was not going to rent one of the high dollar moorings from them. The chart showed an anchorage spot, but there were moorings there too. Finally, we saw an anchored boat near the end of the moorings, so we set the hook there. After a little while, it became clear, that we might swing into others if the wind changed, so we pulled up the anchor and moved back a ways. This time our neighbor yelled over that he would hit us with his boat when the wind changed. We thought we would just wait it out, till an official boat came by to say we would have to move again, which did happen after a while. He kindly gave us directions to go to find the anchorage. We set the hook down the third time, and now we were close to the entrance to the harbor, and the inflowing current had us swinging too close to others again. I was beginning to dislike Nantucket more and more. Farther down the bay there was lots of open water to anchor in, but also shallow water too. We decided to try for it. Motoring around checking depths we found a deep enough hole to anchor in. We had plenty of room to swing, no neighbors to yell at us and free anchorage. The only down side was a 20-minute skiff ride to the dock. We spent the rest of the day relaxing on the boat. Terry having set and pulled the anchor and chain three times, he had done his workout for the day.

The next day, was going ashore day. We got the raft pumped up tight, and we assembled our shore rig, fresh clothes, and stuff for showers, lists of things to look for and look at. We all three climbed in the skiff ready for a good time ashore. Marion hadn't been off the boat since Rockland, about one week ago. Expectations were high. Evidently Mr. 9.9 Johnson had other ideas. He refused to even pop, while

Indian Summer A Sailing Adventure

we pulled and pulled on the cord. Everybody out, this isn't the day we get to shore.

It took Terry and I all day to find that the needle valve in the carburetor had stuck closed not letting the fuel into the engine. By the end of the day, we had the engine running and gave it a good test run around the boat. Surely tomorrow we can go.

I did notice, but tried to ignore the extremely worn pull cord. It was wrapped around a very tight recoil spring and I had bad memories of springs flying apart, never to return to a workable condition again, if I could even keep it from throwing itself into the bay. Working on the Johnson, hanging off the back of the rubber skiff, bouncing around while other boats came roaring by was adding to the difficulty. I sure didn't want to tackle that job. Maybe it would last the rest of the trip, I thought, and I could work on it while the engine was safely on deck.

The next day, we were a little more cautious about hoping to get ashore, so I thought we should give the outboard engine a trial run around the boat before we loaded up again. Good idea, the first pull on the cord broke it clean off before the engine even fired. I guess we now have no options, but to take on the cord replacement. It went better than I expected, we were careful to keep the spring from unraveling when it was removed. I had a replacement cord ready, and in a couple of hours we had the new one installed and on our way into town. The engine was running hot, but we kept going, running slowly towards the dock.

Ashore, we found free showers at the dock. We split up and walked through the town looking at the shops and checking out all there was to see. We had agreed to meet back at the dock at 5:00. We were tired from all the walking and glad to be back at the ship, our home for the summer. Terry had found a map of bike trails on the island and planned to ferry the boat bike ashore the next day. I had found a whaling museum that looked interesting to visit. Marion wanted to take a historic self-guided tour of old houses. We had our tomorrow mapped out.

The next morning, we had Marion get into the skiff first, then lowered the bike on top of her, then Terry and I jumped in and we were off for a fun day in Nantucket. By the end of the day, Terry had covered many miles on the bike in the back country, Marion couldn't find the old house walking trail, but found plenty to look at anyway, and I took in the museum and found out a lot of interesting facts. We met at the grocery store and stocked up for the next leg of the trip. We returned to the boat tired and satisfied with the day. We would leave for Martha's Vineyard the next day.

We got a late start the next day, but we had planned to anchor in the Sound at nightfall. Sailing slow and tacking, took quite some time, and by nightfall, it was clear that stopping in the Sound, would maybe not be the best idea, as there was still a lot of traffic traveling there. It looked like we could make Vineyard Haven Harbor by midnight, and it was very wide, so I thought we could go all the way in, using the chart plotter and radar. The plotter kept us on track and the radar was able to locate the up-coming buoys. The night was warm and pleasant, but very dark with lights shown up in the distance on the mainland and on Martha's Vineyard. There is a lot of shallow water around, so we kept to the main channel, taking no short cuts. We found the entrance to the harbor and followed the buoys in to number six buoy, where we veered off towards the beach. I used my night vision scope to spot other anchored boats, and when we reached a twenty-foot depth I said stop here. We had a few boats anchored nearby, but it looked like we had plenty of swinging room if the wind should come up.

It is always a relief to find a safe spot to stop at, especially when traveling at night, when there can be so many things to go wrong. I almost hated to go to bed, wanting to enjoy the relaxing moment longer. The next day, would be interesting exploring the island. Terry had decided to leave us a day early in order to make good bus connections back to Boston, and his train ride home to Minnesota. Then, it would be just Marion and I running the boat for the next three weeks.

The next day, we all went ashore. Terry would check out ferry service to the mainland and we would explore. We could hang out on this island for at least a week. Terry left the next day and we were sorry to see him go. Terry knew the boat systems well and could single handedly sail the boat in most conditions. It's comforting to have a trusted person at the helm. The day before he left, I had bought a hand primer squeeze pump to flush out the water line in the outboard engine, since it was still running hot. We pulled the skiff up to the shore to install it. There must have been some debris stuck in the line, because on the way back to the boat a lot more water was flowing out the cooling line and the engine was running much cooler as a result.

Terry left on Saturday morning, and Marion and I just poked around the town. The next day, we were invited to supper by some friends of friends we know at home. They live on the island part-time, and heard that we might stop there, so they called us and left a message on our phone. We had arranged to meet at the dock after lunch, so about 12:30 we headed in. We got inside the breakwater and the engine just died. We quickly paddled over to another boat to get out of traffic, where the owners motioned us to tie up. No amount of pulling could get the engine to even pop once. The other boaters, whose boat we were tied to, said they had business at the dock anyway and would tow us in. We met Dave, friend of our friend at the dock, and decided that we would let the motor hang for a while instead of trying to fix it there. I had no tools except my Leatherman anyway, and the way it quit, seemed to indicate something more serious.

We had a great time with our new found friends, Dave had access to a private beach and we had brought along a light lunch and beach gear. We spent a few hours lying around listening to the waves and enjoying the scenery. Later, Dave picked us up and took us to his fishing cabin and to meet his lady friend. She made a terrific meal and we had a good visit, learning about their lives, fishing and boating. We also met Dave's friend, who was featured in the movie Jaws that was filmed here.

It was starting to get dark, and I remembered that the skiff motor was maybe still out of order, so it was time to get back. We got back to the dock at dark and of course the engine refused to fire. Both Dave and I pulled on the cord till we were exhausted. It wouldn't start, not even fire once.

Then as fortune sometimes smiles on us, a friendly boater who was just getting into his skiff, volunteered to drag us out to our boat. I told him we were pretty far out, but he still wanted to help us. I couldn't turn that offer down, so that's how we got back, by his kind help. It never ceases to amaze me how comforting it is to come back to the boat after a day full of adventure. It's such a safe feeling, plus I had my tool box, food and a dry place to sleep. I would look into the motor tomorrow.

In the morning, after a good breakfast, I climbed into the skiff, removed the engine cover and checked for spark, there was none. Then while pulling on some ignition wires, I felt one stuck to the engine head. The engine had been running hot for such a while, that it had melted the wire insulation away causing it to short out. By just wrapping the wire with some leather and tape, the engine ran once again. It made my day. We spent the next few days lying to anchor there, sometimes going ashore and using the fine bus service they have. We found that people over 65, get reduced bus fares and we took advantage of that. Marion, of course, found a flea market to go to, I went too, but didn't buy anything. I had all the jewelry I needed.

I had been studying the tides going through the Woods Hole slot and saw they were very strong. It was important to get the timing right. I am new to this type of navigating and have no one to confer with, so it was with some small degree of satisfaction, that we were sucked right through the slot with a strong current in our favor. Out into Buzzards Bay, we found very light wind, so it's motor time again heading for Mattapoisett, MA.

The weather remained hot the whole way across the bay. We did get some wind towards the end of the run, so we raised some sails. Entering the harbor we found another "mine field" of moorings. Wishing to only anchor, we looked for other anchored boats. Not finding any, we gave the harbor master a call on the radio, no response. So looking up the harbor in my cruising book, I did find a cell phone number to call, which in turn gave me the harbor master's phone number. I guess he does not answer VHF calls. Anyway, he directed me to a place farther into the harbor and told me to pick up a mooring. I repeated my request for an anchorage and got the same directions. Again I asked for a place to anchor, and then was told to go across the bay to Molly's Cove. It was on the chart he said, but it wasn't. We did find it in spite of all this, and set the hook in 15-feet of water at low tide. We drug anchor for a while, till it finally found a spot to dig in.

It was a pleasant place to hang out in, a few boats around, but not much activity. We had about ½-mile to shore, but since the Johnson was working fine, we didn't care. Sometimes it was a little choppy and we landed a little wet, but the days were hot and we dried quickly enough. Mattapoisett didn't have too much to offer a person on foot, a café, library to check e-mail, and charge our phone battery. There was a Laundromat about two miles away, which we walked to and more stores farther out.

One day we tried to catch the bus to Fairhaven, but found the schedules hard to figure out and the stops even harder. We talked to a lady walking her dog about the stops and she wasn't sure where they were either. Later, she came by again in her car and offered us a ride to Walmart as she was going close to there too. We were glad to get a ride after waiting so long. We needed a few things for the boat and I needed to buy some cooler clothes. I had only warm clothes along and had cut off some blue jeans to keep cool. I never wear shorts, but now it was time to start. In one hour we met our new friend and she returned us to the boat dock. She and her husband were also sailors and could guess we were boaters. She knew how difficult it can be, landing in a strange place with no car, trying to pick up supplies. We met some other people too, a couple living full time on their boat, and another couple from Texas vacationing in New Bedford for the summer.

The last day, there was a "Taste of the Town" at the harbor that was interesting. All the local restaurants set up their specialties in a big tent next to the harbor. We bought tickets to sample their goods. Ten dollars gave us enough to try many foods. We also met the two couples we talked with earlier.

I planned to leave the next day for the Cape Cod Canal; however, we had to enter the west end at the turn of the tide and ride the current through the canal. The current was in our favor at 4:00 p.m. It would take us about two to three hours to get through, and after that I wanted to get out into the Cape Cod Bay en route to Provincetown. Of course there is always a hitch to plans.

The forecast was for thundershowers with high winds, lightening and choppy seas that day. The radio had been forecasting that same weather for a couple of days, and I never saw it come to pass, so I thought there would be a good chance the same thing would happen today. We were only two hours away from the canal, so we left the harbor about 1:30 p.m., or so.

As we closed in on the entrance, we saw lightening and dark clouds forming in the west and moving across our path. I hated to abort and go find a place to anchor, so decided to continue the trip. We entered the canal and with sails down began motoring eastward. The wind was light, clouds were dark, and lightening flashed around us. Then this fierce wind came from behind, with blasts of white rain, a complete whiteout. I was going eastward I know at the time. Marion was below watching our movement on the chart plotter. We had the main hatch closed, but the hatch boards were out so she could yell to me our position. In this complete whiteout, she was yelling that I was going backwards. This I couldn't believe. I still felt the wind and rain on my back, and a look at the water over the side, didn't show me backing up. Once in a while, I could just make out the shapes of the right and left buoy markers. I knew I was still in the channel and didn't want to lose sight of them, and be blown off into shallow water, and become stuck in a mud bank. Finally, she said I was going back to where we came from, in other words, west. We had been blown completely around without my knowing it. I had to believe her now. Blindly I turned the boat around and cautiously began motoring, what I had thought was the wrong way. I wasn't really convinced, until I could see the highway bridge crossing the canal ahead. I knew that we had not passed under it before. Marion passed some dry clothes up to me, as I was soaked to the skin and freezing. I wanted to keep motoring, as the current had us in its grip and it was constantly sluing the boat around.

We got to the east end of the canal at dark, and found very rough seas. The current had now reversed, and we were bucking the remaining outflowing current. Motoring hard, we barely made any forward motion, but kept at it for a couple of hours, before we found some calmer water. Raising some sails, we just drifted northward.

Later that night, Marion had gone to bed, and I was getting very tired from the earlier stress and needed to get some rest. *Indian Summer,* can lay hove-to, by trimming the sails to essentially park the boat in the water. We will drift slowly downwind. There were a few ships coming out of the canal, but they all seemed to be heading to the Boston area. I lit the kerosene lantern, hung it as high as I could reach on the stern deck and laid down for a much needed rest. Little did I know how trying tomorrow would be, or I would have motored all night, to get as close to P-Town, before the adverse wind came up.

Early in the morning, I woke and checked our position. We hadn't made any progress toward P-Town, and worse, a northeast wind had come up, our exact course. Sailing to windward is rough going, and requires us to sail well off our course, covering many extra miles to gain a few. We pitched and rolled along for hours, and seemed to get nowhere. I finally had to start the engine again, drop the head sail, reef the main sail, and punch right into the waves. Doing this we can normally motor sail to within 10 degrees of the wind. The wind was strong enough to put up four-to five-foot seas and it was a little wet at times, water coming over the bow and thrown back by the wind, sometimes the boat would be hit so hard by a wave, we would completely stop. When we got closer to The Cape, the waves became smaller and we made better progress. Around 10 a.m., we came to anchor in the harbor at Provincetown. I cannot tell you how great the feeling is, to finally anchor the boat in a secure place, and be able to crawl into a warm bunk with no worries. We slept most of the day and it was wonderful.

I had thought of sailing closer to Boston, after we had seen Provincetown. We had friends in Hull and Boston we could visit, but the wind was forecast to blow out of the west in two days, and the outgoing current would greet us late in the afternoon, while trying to get into Hull. Also, it was a 36-mile sail, one day sailing to get there, and after Bruce and Chuck came, we would have to retrace our path, another day sail back to where we were now, or close to it. It didn't make sense to move from this harbor. We could just relax and enjoy the area, I was sure we could find plenty to do if we wanted.

We went ashore many times, found some good eating

places, a good library to check e-mail and charge our phone battery, a large grocery store and even a thrift store for Marion.

A couple of days after arriving at Provincetown, I was idly looking for something to do on the boat and I just happened to look in the bilge. I have a swing plate in the floor right above the sump pocket in the bilge. I was sure it would be dry as I have a horn rigged up to sound if more than five gallons come in. To my horror the whole bilge was full, only a few inches from the floorboards. I knew we were a long way from sinking, but where was the water coming from? I instantly began thinking of worst case scenario. Bruce and Chuck are coming in a few days. If I have to haul out to make repairs, that could take a week or more, plus I have no idea where to do this. I would have to sail somewhere else. Or maybe we are taking in water now faster than I can clear it. Marion had taken some sewing project up on the foredeck and was not aware of my panic attack. I had to force myself not to say anything yet, till I had more information. I began pumping the water overboard and realized how dependent I was on that small plastic pump. If it broke, I didn't have a backup pump to replace it. I would add that to my spare parts list before the next cruise. I pumped till my arms ached, stopped, rested and pumped again. It took quite some time before I saw results in the way of dropping water levels. Then I knew I was going to clear it, if the pump didn't break first. While pumping, I was thinking of possible sources of the leak. Since I had personally built the boat, I knew that there are only seven holes under the waterline. I would have to check them all out. After 45 minutes of pumping, I heard the welcome sucking sound. We were dry again.

Now I pulled the floorboards up and wiped all the areas dry that had sea cocks plugging the holes, they were OK. Then I checked the prop shaft area, dry, the rudder shaft, dry, the cockpit drains, dry. No water was coming in anywhere. Well, good news there, but will something open up when Marion and I were ashore? I replaced the floorboards and let Marion down into the cabin. She had had enough sun. When she came down, I told her we had a little water in the boat, but had it cleared. I said maybe we had pulled in water through the rudder shaft hole on the trip across the bay a few days earlier. I had that happen once before, but had since replaced the seal with a much better system. Maybe it was still a problem?

This mystery bothered me for a few days, till one day, I was looking at the sink drain and suddenly realized where the water had come from. The sink drain is only about six inches above the waterline. When we are plunging in the sea, hydraulic water pressure is created in the drain hole and back filled through the pump into the bilge. Now I remembered that I had this problem before, and had put a shutoff valve in the line to prevent this. What a relief to finally understand the problem, so simple. Now in rough going we just close the sink valve. Originally I had a separate drain for the bilge, but on our ocean crossing, the bilge pump had broken and we rigged the sink pump as the bilge pump. In the past four years I had forgotten this minor detail.

That was maybe the most excitement of our anchorage there, and I'm glad of that. Also, while anchored there, some friends from Hull came by ferry to visit us. We had them out to the boat for a meal, and later walked through the shopping center. One from the group, Joey McDonnell, had sailed with us across the North Sea from Norway to the Shetland Islands.

This was the first time since then, he had been aboard. He enjoyed showing his girlfriend and brother the boat and where his bunk was. It had been a rough passage and we had been tested as only the North Sea could do.

We had other friends come over from Boston and the Cape; Anna, Blake, Andy and Berry. We had known Anna since she was in the fifth grade with our daughter, and attended her wedding with Blake last year. Her father, John, came out to Maine this year to help me get the boat ready for the sailing season. We had met Andy and Berry, Blake's parents last year, it was so nice of them to pay us a visit.

A couple of things we did in Provincetown were to hike to the museum at the base of Pilgrim Monument, a 252-foot tower built in the years 1907 to 1910. The museum was very interesting with much information on early life on the Cape, plus a very informative video on the tower. No, we didn't hike to the top, but one could have. I'm sure the view was worth it. We ate a few times at the Portuguese Bakery, shopped a bit at a store, selling left over debris from Army-Navy goods to airline coffee cups and everything in between. There is quite a gay scene in P-Town and gives one something to look at too. To each his own I won't judge. A number of street musicians and mimes rounded out the entertainment.

Sometimes we stayed a bit later than we should have. It made for an interesting ride back to the boat, having now turned very dark, and *Indian Summer,* on the outskirts of the harbor with no lights on. We motored in what we thought would be the right direction and were so glad to find our boat in that darkness.

After a little over a week lying to anchor, Bruce and Chuck arrived on schedule, Saturday evening. They wanted to go directly to the boat, no interest in touring the town. We had a good supper and turned in early, wanting to get a good start in the morning. The winds were forecasted to be northeast the next day and later veering eastward. Not the best direction for starters, but promised to get better as the week went on.

To leave the anchorage, we had a fair wind around the curve part of The Cape, but in a couple of hours we had the foul wind on the nose. It wasn't strong, but we made very slow progress, and by late in the evening, we only had P-Town on the starboard beam. Bruce had done some steering early on, but now was laid out in the cockpit with sea sickness. He had quit talking and made frequent visits to the rail. I could empathize with him, having been seasick a few times myself. I hoped that he would recover before we landed, so he could enjoy some sailing. Chuck was holding his own, but still couldn't eat. Chuck and I changed off steering through the night.

That night, we had whales surface next to the boat and sometimes dive right under us. They did have me worried, that a bump on the rudder would knock our steering out of whack, but they were careful enough and made no contact with our boat. A few attempts trying to take pictures of them gave us only pictures of the sea. I thought about my visit to the whaling museum in Nantucket, and wondered at the courage of whalers that would harpoon a whale at such a close range. It must have been quite a rush. I thought, no thanks, I don't need that much excitement.

During the early hours, we entered the traffic separation zone for ships going into Boston. This zone requires ships to stay in their proper lane, depending on inbound or outbound course. The wind was still light, so we started the engine to get across. Small boats can cross at right angles and it's no time to dally, we made it across with no incident.

By Monday morning sunrise, we were well offshore. It's always exciting to see the sun rise up out of the sea. The new crew was still dealing with seasickness and not eating anything. Bruce still made dives for the rail, but had nothing more to give up. Chuck had finally thrown up and now felt better, but still didn't dare eat much. The day proved to be totally lacking in wind and hot. We drifted slowly northward. The forecast, wind from the east, failed to appear. After a time, I decided that motoring might be required to get the crews hopes up, that we would ever see land again. Had there been no bus and plane tickets bought for the return home of the crew, I would have waited for some wind, but schedules must be maintained if possible. I started the engine.

By nightfall, the wind had come at last and we were sailors again. Chuck had his sea legs now and was enjoying the cruise. Bruce was also on the road to recovery and up out of his comatose state. When I came on deck to take my turn at the helm, I saw the boat moving fast, but could tell that Chuck was having a workout on the wheel. The boat was carrying too much main sail, causing the boat to slew around. He would catch it in time, but sooner or later we were going to broach, i.e. be thrown sideways. Not good in a following sea.

I hated to do a main sail reef with Bruce and Chuck in these conditions, but it had to be done. I kept Chuck on the wheel, and explained how he would turn us into the wind to get the pressure off the sail. Also, to expect a lot of pitching and rolling as we headed directly into the waves. Bruce would stay in the cockpit and lower the main halyard, while I would be at the foot of the mast pulling down some of the sail. When I had enough sail down, I would attach the lower corner of the sail, the tack, and yell to Bruce to lock down the halyard, and pull in the reef line at the end of the boom over his head. Then Chuck could turn downwind again and we would have the boat balanced again. I had Chuck do a trial turn just to see how much motion to expect. He needed to select the right time to make the turn, not just as a wave was making behind us. When this was done we were ready for the real thing.

Now, I know this can go smoothly or it can go oh-so-badly. If someone gets an arm or leg trapped in a coil of line, being pulled by the wind and thrown overboard, it can be a nightmare. The boat is disabled at the time and too many problems to deal with at once. We were ready for the test. Chuck made the turn, Bruce let go the halyard, I pulled in the required sail, hitched the clew, and Bruce locked the halyard down and pulled in the reef line. It went so smoothly, except a furling line snarled in the reef line, kept the reef line from totally pulling in the sail. We gave it another try, but it was jammed. I didn't want to press our luck any farther. The boat was sailing fine now, with the reduced sail, even with a jammed reef line. It made the boat so much easier to steer and safer too.

Bruce and Chuck retired below, while I took my turn at the wheel. It was sometime during the night, on my shift, we struck something on the bow. The boat shuttered and came to a complete stop. Chuck came up immediately wondering what we hit. I don't know, I said. It felt like we ran aground, but we were about 15-miles from the nearest island and in 200-feet of water. No water was coming in the bilge, and soon the wind got hold of our sails, and we were off again, no damage.

By Tuesday morning, we had Matinicus Rock in sight. I had thought that we wouldn't be close enough to any island to anchor Tuesday night. I had planned to lay hove-to, through the night and continue on to Stonington, Maine, on Wednesday, where we had left our car six weeks before. As we got closer to the off laying islands of Maine, the lobster traps would become denser. It would be too easy to drift into them at night, snarling the lines in our rudder and prop. We had to stop before we got too close to them. When I measured the distance to Moores Harbor in Isle au Haut, I found that if we could maintain four knots through the day, we could be in Moore Harbor before nightfall. We used both engine and sail to keep our speed up and made good progress to the harbor.

We found the harbor OK, but it was a little trouble finding a spot to drop anchor. We eventually settled on an area that looked good after circling a few times watching the depth finder. We were happy to be stopped for the night and in a scenic spot to boot. There was another sailboat anchored a little ways from us and they had just run their dog ashore. On the way back to the boat, they stopped by to say hello. By now everyone had their sea legs and appetite, so Marion made us a good supper. It looked like a raining night, so we rigged up the forward canvas cover over the hatch, and put up mosquito netting, as they were coming out after the sun went down.

By morning, we had rain and fog, but decided to move out anyway in hopes that things would clear up. The weather did clear up shortly, and since we were only 11 miles from Stonington, we got there early in the day. After looking over the public dock with binoculars, I saw that there wasn't enough room for us at the dock, as there was another boat already there. Bruce and Chuck assembled the skiff and hung the motor for the ride ashore. I took Bruce, Chuck and Marion to the dock and came back to the boat for a nap. The crew would sample Stonington cuisine at the Harbor Café and I was just happy to spend some more time aboard my boat, knowing that soon, we would be putting her away for the winter.

At the agreed time, I returned to the dock to pick up crew. They had all had a great meal of sea food and were in high spirits. Bill and Wendy came down to see us. Marion would be spending the night at their house. Tomorrow she would spend driving and shopping on the way up to our new marina at Winterport, while we sailed there. We hauled in the motor and skiff when we got back to the boat. We were ready to leave early the next day.

Of course it was foggy when we got up, and slowly it burned off. We made good use of the plotter again, keeping us on the track. We still had someone on the bow looking for lobster traps, while another steered, and another watching the plotter and radar below. We managed to keep off most of the traps, only snagging two of them all the way up. We anchored off Fort Point for the night, and would have to catch the upriver current in the morning. The current can run at six knots, so it could prove to be a fast trip upriver to the new marina.

In the morning, the fog was dense, barely able to see off the side of the boat. We had to start out though, if we wanted to catch the current. By now, we had our positions of bow watcher, helmsman and plotter/radar watchman. We motored through the fog, not meeting any boats and about ¾ hour later, we passed under the main highway bridge and were mainly in the river system and out of the bay. The fog was lifting by now and we had good visibility. The current had us, and we made good speed over the ground. By 10:30, we had made Winterport and slid into the dock. I had not been able to reach them in person, but had left a message saying when we would be there. The last time I talked to the owners was in early June, so I was happy to hear one of the employees say they had been expecting us, as he tied up our lines.

Trying to keep bus, train and plane schedules while on a sailboat can be quite a challenge, but this time all worked out. It reminded me of a sailor Marion and I met a few years ago in Spain. He told us that when picking up or dropping off crew, he would give them either time or a place, but never the two at once, maybe good advice to keep in mind.

Indian Summer was hauled out the following Monday, we had arrived Friday morning. She was pressure washed and after some repairs to the haul out trailer, set down Tuesday on stands. I was anxious to clean out the boat of all the gear we no longer needed. It had been 12 years since we had a chance to haul much stuff home, the boat being in Europe and too difficult to take much home on the plane. Marion did a super job of packing the little Toyota and we barely had room to sit. By Wednesday morning, we had paid our bill, winterized the boat, and locked her up. We were away by 10:00 a.m., and it did feel good to be heading home with a successful summer sailing over.

2013 Sailing Adventures in Maine

In early April, I left Wannaska for a Mayo, regular

doctor checkup in Rochester MN. From there, I would head east for Yorkville, IL, to spend a night with Marion's brother and sister-in-law. Then keep going to Boston, and then north to Winterport, ME, where I keep the boat. John Carstens had again agreed to drive out and help me get the boat ready for the coming season.

We met at Yorkville, and spent the night there, enjoyed some good hospitality, and in the morning, Paul took us out for breakfast. We left after breakfast and drove around Chicago and east towards Cleveland, then turned and drove down through Pennsylvania, coming through Hartford and into Boston. We spent one night sleeping in our cars before reaching Boston.

While en route, I got another call from a young lady wanting to know more about the sailing trip I had advertised about in the local paper. I told her that this year, we would be just sailing close to the coast and anchoring every night with some exploring trips ashore. I suggested that she find a friend to come with her, as it would only be Marion and I on the boat. I said that there would be lots of time not sailing, so she needed to have other interests like reading, photography and such. Later she did call back and said that she had a boyfriend who wanted to go. I was not too sure this was a good idea. Luckily, later she declined to come, whew.

Earlier, I had ran an ad in the paper looking for anyone interested in sailing on the coast of Maine, no cost and no experience required. I had received quite a few calls and had selected three to come. One was to come earlier and the other two later, and only for a week or so. There was another fellow who was anxious to experience a few days of sailing, and I gave him dates that where available, but at the last minute, he could only come when I had others already signed to come, he dropped out. Marion had at first decided not to come sailing this summer, but later changed her mind. In that case, it was not too important if I took on crew or not, as Marion and I do just fine on our own.

We arrived in Boston at Anna and Blake Mensing's, John's daughter. We spent a few days there, and it was cool yet, so there is no hurry to get to the boat. I had picked up a bad cough and was happy to take a little time to recover. We left Boston about noon, the day of the Boston Marathon, and drove north in a nice sunny day. It was good to get away from all the traffic, and about three hours later, while pulling into a gas station, we heard of the bombings at the marathon. So glad we got out of there when we did, as the bombings had happened close to where we had been staying, a mile or so away.

The boat had been moved a little from where we had left it last year, but still very close to electric power. The primary projects this year will be; to paint the deck, treat any rusting areas under the waterline, paint on two coats of antifouling, (it takes three gallons for this), move the throttle over from the cockpit side panel to the pedestal, and install a LED light in the main cabin. Besides these projects, we were able to sand, treat, and paint the bulkhead in the vee bunk, clean up the nav. station, since I had removed the ham radio and gear, it left a big hole and a mess of wires, made the forward sink operational, painted the floor and steps. We also reinstalled the wheel and ran up the running rigging. All this took about three weeks to do and by the end of April, John headed back to Boston to meet up with his wife and the trip home. I got a taxi to come get me May 6, for a ride to Bangor Airport and the flight home. This time I would fly right to Grand Forks instead of the bus ride from Minneapolis to Grand Forks, poor connections made me wait hours at the bus station in Minneapolis.

I worked in my shop for about a month and got enough work done to justify coming home for such a short time. On May 31, we drove down to Delano, Mary and Bruce's home, and spent the night. The next day, Saturday, we went to Bruce's graduation ceremony, and drove back to Little Falls to take in Marion's cousin's, daughter's wedding. Later, I drove back north to Grand Forks, to spend the night at Erin and Brad's house and catch the return flight to Bangor. Marion would fly out of Minneapolis to Portland via stops in between and then take the bus to Bangor. Our arrival times in Bangor were about the same, so we rode the same taxi back to Winterport.

We arrived at the boat June 6, and still had a few last minute things to do before launch. The cabin was still full of gear, and a lot of it could be stored in the car for the summer. We had to clean cupboards, hang sails, and buy groceries. We got the boat launched on Thursday, and the first crew, Steve Johnson from Malung, came on Friday. We drove to the airport that night to get him, the plane was late and we had a long wait. Steve arrived with two bags, one huge with a lot of rain gear, boots etc. Back at the boat we found places for all. Boats can sleep a lot of people, it's the gear we all need along that takes up room.

We left on Sunday, giving Steve a last minute chance to buy things, he didn't need it. We sailed to Fort Point and found an unused mooring to hook up to. I always hate to use someone else's mooring. It's like parking in their garage, but by morning no one kicked us off and we sailed on. Next stop was Warren Island.

We sailed south first, to enter the Penobscot Bay, then

to the west toward Belfast. The wind was giving us a beam reach, our fastest point of sail. We soon were sailing south, down the west side of the bay. The wind being from the south, made us tack from shore to shore, and the wind seemed to be letting up some.

On one tack, we had just turned and hadn't picked up speed yet, when the strangest thing happened. I was steering with Steve sitting to port, Marion was in the cabin. Suddenly, with no sense of wind, the boat started to slowly heel over and over and over. I heard things crashing down below in the cabin. I at first thought that we had ran aground and the wind was pushing us over, but a quick jerk on the main sheet cleat, reduced the wind pressure and brought us upright, and we were moving again. Steve was getting a little concerned and I was wondering, what the heck was that? From Marion, not a sound was heard. I guess she figured that's all part of the adventure, she's amazing!

We came to anchor just before dark, having started the engine the last three miles, as the wind had quit for us. Well, not really to anchor, but picked up a free mooring, and settled in for a nice quite night. We would explore the island tomorrow.

The next day started out calm. We were so close to the dock, it seemed that we could just paddled in, not taking time to hang the ten horse Johnson motor. Marion had made lunch for us each to take along. Right off the dock, there is an information booth with a box to drop money in. I paid for the three of us and we started off on the trails. We agreed to check in, via our ham radio hand held at certain times, so Steve walked on ahead of us.

We just dallied and spent a little time talking to a couple of rangers before getting into the interior of the island.

The trails are well kept and easy to walk, some uphill. There are lots of places to stop for picnics. I had planned to take John, Sara and Mallori here later, and was interested to check it out. We did a few trails and stopped at noon for our lunch. We met up with Steve, on the last trail back to the dock. We met some campers not far from the dock, pitching tents and cooking. We didn't get invited to stay for supper, but it would have been nice to stay and visit.

The wind had picked up by now, and it was too dangerous to paddle back to the boat. Now it seemed much farther away, with lots of rough water between us, than this morning when it was so still and calm. We waited maybe a couple of hours and the wind started to go down some. Also, there were nasty storm clouds heading our way that sure looked like rain. I decided that all three of us would get ready to shove off in the first lull and paddle like crazy, which we did. We made it to the boat just before the rain and wind hit with a vengeance. We're glad we weren't camping or waiting on the dock. It was nice and snug in the cabin. The next day, we headed south around the east side of Warren Island and over to Camden.

We entered Camden Harbor and started looking for a place to anchor. I didn't feel like renting a mooring, as I knew they would be a bit expensive. We needed to find a place outside of the mooring fields and out of the way of the traffic lane. It seemed like there were no real good choices, but having picked a likely looking spot, I had Steve drop the anchor. I backed the boat down trying to get the anchor to grab, but the farther I backed down, the closer to the traffic lane we got. Well, nothing else to do, but try again. Steve and I started to pull up the anchor. When we got it up, he was worn out and suggested to buy a mooring. He would pay for it. This was just the first time we had pulled anchor and I sure don't give up that fast. We looked for another spot. The second drop felt better when we backed down on the anchor, so I called it good.

We spent the night at anchor and the next day we made plans to go ashore. It was a little windy, but not dangerously so. Steve surprised us in saying he would stay on the boat. That's OK. It never hurts to have an anchor watch while we're ashore. We agreed to keep in touch via VHF ham radio. Marion and I took the skiff into the dock. We spent a little time walking through the town, stopped at a thrift store, used book store and the library.

While at the library, I checked in with Steve, and he thought the anchor was slipping some and we should come back real soon. Marion was not too happy, as she hadn't had time to check out the stores properly. We took the skiff back to the boat and prepared to leave Camden. I'm not so sure we had dragged. It can be hard to judge if the boat swings, but at any rate, we were ready to go. Heading out of Camden Harbor we sailed east for Pulpit Harbor. I had never been there before, but the chart made it seem very interesting. It looked like a small body of water with only a narrow entrance. I thought it would be fun to look it over.

We arrived there in the afternoon and dropped anchor. It was a bit foggy on the way over. On approach to the bay, we had what looked like a choice of passing on either side of Pulpit Rock. However, on close examination of the chart, we saw that the north side is the proper way in. After anchoring during high tide we watched as rocks started to appear on the right or south side, making for a very rough entrance to the bay. After getting squared away for the evening, Steve wanted to know what was here. These islands are mainly just places for summer cabins. Maybe there are a few year-round residents, if lucky, a convenience store with limited items for sale. Most of the places we visit are not developed and we look forward to visiting them for that reason, besides the challenge to get there under sail.

The next day, we went ashore, Marion had packed light lunches for us and we decided to go at our own pace. Steve went on ahead. Marion and I just drifted along with a small convenience store as our goal. The road was paved and narrow.

About an hour of hiking brought us to Mid-Island Grocery. We met Steve there, who had hiked all over the immediate area and would go back to the skiff. Marion & I went inside the store for ice cream. We visited outside with a fifth grade teacher and met his two kids. Later, we would meet people who knew him, as we crossed the island south of here. We were keeping in touch with Steve by ham radio, and he was already at the skiff. He said he could motor closer to our location and pick us up saving us a long walk back.

On the way back, we visited a cemetery and wondered at the people buried there. A lot of families in a family plot, makes you wonder at the lives they lead while here. We arrived at the commercial dock for fisherman and Steve was there. He ran us back to the boat and we made plans to sail on to Castine. I plotted the course on the chart plotter and got things ready for the morning.

The next day, on leaving, the tide was lower than when we came in. The rocks on the south side of Pulpit Rock showed up very prominent. There is also a mud bank in the middle of the track to the exit, so we had to swing around this bank. Once clear of the entrance, we had a good run north.

We came into Castine Harbor and turned north into Smith Cove to anchor. There were quite a few boats here, but plenty of room to anchor.

The next day, while getting ready to head into town, Steve decided to stay aboard. He had walked so much that he got blisters on his feet, besides, I don't think he thought too much of exploring these islands. I sure didn't mind, it's nice to have someone on anchor watch. In anchoring, there will always be a time when it slips out, due to change in wind direction, wind force or tidal change. Also, sometimes the chain can get hooked around the nose of the anchor and prevent it from digging in.

In Castine, we tied up the skiff and asked the harbor master if it was OK to leave it there. He said it would be OK for a couple of hours. I guess they don't need people to stay too long. We did get our water jugs filled though. The town didn't have too much for a downtown.

We hiked to the Maritime College, and the site of a British Fort. A very important battle was fought near here, the Battle of 1779. It's listed as the biggest defeat to the US Navy, second only to Pearl Harbor. It seems that the British had started to build up a fort here and the US Navy, commanded by John Paul Jones, with the Marines and the Army from Boston, was sent to kick them out. They lay at anchor just outside Castine, and had a much superior force to the British, but there was infighting, as to who would go in first. They dallied for a few days, while the British came up the bay with many ships. This forced the Americans to burn their own ships, to keep the British from getting them. Then the Americans had to march overland back to Boston in defeat. Chalk that one up to the Brits.

After Castine, we sailed across the top of the bay to

Belfast to let Steve off. He had decided that he would take a bus back to Bangor a day early.

We stayed at Belfast a few days, finding it was a good place to stock up on groceries and do laundry. They have an around town bus service, that was poorly advertised. They ran three days a week, till one o'clock, for a fee of one dollar per person. What a bargain! Instead of lugging groceries a mile up and down the big hill by the harbor. We met a very helpful person at the information place, Debbie Reynolds, and we ran into her later and became friends. She was buying some property and was anxious to tell us about it, and even drove us out of town to look it over. She had dreams of building a small house on it someday; we hope she can make it come true.

After Belfast, we sailed for Holbrook Island. We had first heard of the island from an information place in Castine. The lady there told us it was off limits to go ashore, but later while talking with a sail maker in Belfast, he highly recommended it. He even said there were free moorings there. We were going to find out.

Coming into the bay, we were lured over to the opposite side by a group of moorings. In my careless moment, I almost ran us aground on a mud bank. It was covered while we sailed in. At the last minute, I looked at the chart plotter and saw we were headed right across a shallow bank. I quickly made a course change and rounded up into the mooring basin. A lot of the moorings were marked private or else just a number. It didn't have the welcome letters that say visitor.

Across the bay, we saw with the binoculars another lone mooring next to a pontoon dock. We motored over to check it out and it was what we had been looking for. A small open boat was tied up to the dock. We grabbed on to the mooring and soon had us tied up for the night. We hiked all through the island and appreciated the well-kept trails. We met two college boys who were doing mowing there. We didn't find any big sand beaches, but plenty of stony ones. The inland trails were dark, dense with small trees. It would be something straight out of the Hansel and Gretel story.

We spent two nights on the mooring and finally it was time to sail to Searsport. We had heard that they have a good Fourth of July celebration, and it was a place we could sail to.

We anchored off the breakwater pretty much in the open. It might get a little rough, but the holding was good and we didn't have any close neighbors to bump into. We got there on the third and thought we would just walk around a bit. We stopped into the Penobscot Museum and met Maggie, a lady who works there. She gave us a lot of good information as to what would be going on tomorrow. There would be a Revolutionary reenactment; the museum was free that day, an auction, book sale, some vendors and a parade. Sounded like fun. I asked about the nearest gas station, as our fuel for the skiff was low. She offered to give us a ride over after work, as it was quite a ways to walk.

The next day, we came in and took in the auction, bought some books, and bought a BBQ chicken lunch. We saw the parade and later Marion found a garage sale. I bought some cheap bags to haul mainly groceries in. We sat and listened to some music at the park. Finally, it was time to go. It seems that while on foot, two or three days about covers the area. Searsport was a good place to buy groceries, as the store was not too far from the dock and there was good water right at the dock too. Next stop would be Stonington, with a stopover off some island.

227

We had a nice sail south, and found a likely island to anchor next to. We lowered the sails and motored in closer. The nearer we came to the island, the more lobster pots we found. They have a nasty habit of winding their rope around the prop shaft and sometimes doing damage to the prop shaft. Also, they can be very hard to get free of, so we try to find a place free of them, good luck.

It seems like when I find a spot in the open and get the hook down, we have drifted into a field of pots, so it's up anchor and try again. Finally, we got hooked in, and in a little closer to shore than I wanted, but thought it would be OK, if we didn't drag, it's always a possibility. It was getting closer to dark and no time to go ashore to explore. However, I did spy with the binoculars, two signs nailed to a couple of trees and my curiosity got the best of me, I had to find out what they said.

I untied the skiff and ran up to the beach. It was a stony beach, about two hundred yards long. On the two trees were the two signs I saw from the boat. One was a name of the beach, Orchard Beach, on the other sign, was information stating that this was a private island, but the owners did permit visitors to land on the beach only during the day, no fires allowed and take garbage with you when you leave, that sounded fair enough. There is an organization that maintains a string of islands, beaches in Maine and we were encouraged to join.

We spent the night anchored off Butter Island, and once in a while, bumped into the pot floats as the boat swung back and forth with the changing of the current. I would have to sort out the mess of lines when we left, too late to do anything tonight. In the morning we motored ashore to do some beachcombing. Marion found more rocks to use as ballast for the boat, till we haul out in the fall. Then we'll haul the rocks back to Minnesota. I wonder if Mainers who visit Minnesota gather up our rocks here and haul them back to Maine.

After the beachcombing, we motored back to the boat and raised anchor. I was expecting a tangle of anchor rode and lobster pot lines, but I was surprised when all came up free. We motored out into the open water and with Marion steering us into the wind, I raised the main and jib sail. We were on the way to Stonington.

It was a bright, sunny day with a fair wind. The closer we got to Stonington, the more familiar everything seemed. We gave Bill McDonnell a call to let him know we would be anchored off Stonington that afternoon. Bill is a brother to Joe, a close neighbor and good friend of ours here in Northern Minnesota. Bill was glad to hear that we would be in town, and offered a spare mooring of his, right in the harbor, next to where he moors his boat, *Nanatoo*. This was good news, as not only is it hard to find a good anchorage sometimes, but pulling up the anchor is very hard work. There is a forty-five pound anchor, attached to fifty-five feet of 3/8 chain and one hundred fifty feet of heavy rode to pull up manually, it's a workout.

We came to Stonington about mid-afternoon, and after some study of the many boats and moorings anchored there, decided that this empty mooring would be the one he meant for us to use. I sure didn't want to be scolded by some stranger for using his mooring.

After a while, Bill arrived with his boat. He works on an off island, and now rowed over in his skiff. It was so nice to see him and we were anxious to visit with him and his wife, Wendy, again. Wendy owns the dental office here in

Stonington and they are so glad to have her there. We arranged to meet them at the local café, Harbor Café, for supper the next day, our treat. We spent the night there and the next day, we walked around the town looking into all the shops. We met Bill and Wendy as planned and had a great supper. Marion and I had lobster, a real treat for Minnesotans. We all left stuffed and caught up on the past events on the island. We made plans to leave in the morning.

The next morning, revealed a thick fog; departure time was delayed for clearer weather. Towards noon, the fog cleared somewhat, maybe one-half mile visibility, so I decided we could leave. I had located a good looking spot within our cruising range for the day, called Johns Island. From the chart, it showed a little bay with protection from the prevailing winds. We dropped the mooring line and motored off. The wind was too light for sails. The fog never let up totally and after a while we were in the soup. The chart plotter was the only thing keeping us on course. We could see no land. We had to constantly keep a watch for lobster pots and turning to avoid snagging them with the skeg. We blindly followed the chart plotter course, turning on many different headings to clear rock islands marked on the chart. Of course the wind picked up, making it harder to stay on course, but we were able to raise some sail. We had a buoy marker close to our anchorage spot, and were glad when it passed close to port. We arrived at our anchorage seeing nothing but fog, no land to be seen.

Right off the bow, we found we were in a minefield of lobster pots. I had Marion steer the boat, while I conned from the bow, looking for a clear spot to set the anchor. In water deep enough to keep us off the bottom at low water, but not so deep to make anchoring difficult. I located a likely spot and let the anchor and chain rattle down. Marion reversed the prop, and we backed down till we felt the boat stop and start to swing off to the side. We were still too close to some pots, but I thought it would have to do for now. I was so glad to be stopped and all in one piece. Looking off the boat, we could only see fog, although the chart said we were less than one quarter mile from Johns Island. We spent a pleasant evening there, and in the morning, the fog had cleared and sure enough, there was Johns Island. We were in no hurry to leave, and the anchor was holding well, so we stayed another day there.

We were close to Casco Passage, an opening in the string of islands we were on. We watched as some boats passed through the passage, did some reading and just lazing around. Time passes and the next thing we know, it's the next day and time to leave.

Our destination was the west end of Mount Desert Island, to a place called Seal Cove. We got the boat ready to cruise again, putting everything away, clearing off the counters, checking the fuel, oil on the engine, and plotting our course to Seal Cove. I like to reach each new anchorage with enough daylight to get settled in proper. We marked off the miles and calculated the time we had for sailing before pulling up anchor. Marion will help steer the boat when we first get going so I can pull up the anchor and raise the sails. Actually, I have a new way of hauling up the anchor now that involves both of us, but that came later after a near disaster, I'll explain further on in this trip. So Marion motors us up to the anchor, while I'm pulling in the loose rode. When we are right over the anchor, I cinch off the anchor line and let the swell that's rising and lowering the boat, pull the anchor out of the mud. Then its heave-ho to get the rest of the fifty-five feet of chain and forty-five pound anchor on deck. If we are clear of any danger, Marion will come forward and help pull it in. It's a chore. Then, while I clean off the mud on the line, and stow away the anchor and rode, she motors us off to the first way point. I have normally given her a course to steer. When all is up and running, sails set and all put away, I will usually take the wheel.

We are around the buoy and into the bay, surprised at all the lobster pots and lobster boats in action. We count seven at one time. It sounds like Grand Central Station with all the motors racing to get to the next pot to check. It's a bright sunny day and we are lucky to be there. Passing through a low string of islands, we notice a couple of houses built on them. There is hardly a tree to see on them. The chart showed a buoy marking the starb'd side of the passage through them and a lot of shallow water all around. It isn't till we are actually passing through the passage that we see the marker. We are where we should be. Crossing over the last bay, tacking back and forth, we arrive at Seal Cove in good light. There are a few boats moored there, maybe thirty or so. I find a spot outside of the moored boats and we go through the anchor routine again, the anchor sticks solid after backing a bit further than I had planned, but we are OK, just a little close to an unoccupied mooring float. Time to relax again, we'll go ashore tomorrow.

We take the skiff in to shore and find a launch area for small craft and a paved road. On inquiring as to any place of interest to hike to, we are told that nothing within walking distance would be available. We did talk with a man from Florida, who was on some kind of church vacation, and also with a couple from New York, who have a pull-type RV and are living the summer near here at Bar Harbor. The man was kayaking and we visited for a while when he came ashore. I hiked a mile or so down the road and talked with a man waiting in a bus that had a trailer hooked behind. He had dropped off a group of kayakers and was waiting to pick them up as they paddled along the coast. There wasn't much to hang around for, so we decided to shove off the next day. We would head up north, through the Eggemoggin Reach, and find a nice island to anchor off to. Our goal would be to arrive back in Belfast for a Celtic celebration. It promised to be a good time and we have been looking forward to it for weeks. Little did we know it would be the time of near disaster for us?

The next day, we pulled up anchor at noon with a light southerly wind and sunny. Marion steered us out of the anchorage, while I put away the anchor gear and raised all sails, main, stays'l and genoa sail. Many lobster pots to dodge, we did snag one, but were able to shake it loose. The wind picked up strength and we tacked back and forth to maintain our course.

There are so many interesting islands that we sail by, and I thought it would be nice to stop early and explore one. I saw an island called Mahoney Island and it looked clear of off lying rocks, so we started to motor in close. Marion was steering a course I had given her, while I lowered away the sails and got the anchor gear ready.

As we got closer, I noticed some submerged rocks that I didn't think should be there. I went below to consult the chart and to my horror we were heading to a different island, Smuttynose Island. There were many rocks listed on the chart. We did a quick turn around and I suddenly lost my adventuresome spirit. We went back to our original plan. I had planned to arrive at our destination about 3:00 p.m., and due to so many islands looking the same, I had sailed past the one I had wanted. On closer examination I saw a few too many rocks lying just off shore, having been spooked earlier, so I picked another island up ahead, Torrey Island. We dropped all sail and motored in slowly checking the depth with the electronic depth finder. A lot handier than a weight and a line, but I do have it in reserve, in case the electronic one quits.

We came to anchor in 30 feet and no lobster pots around. I wonder if that always means mud bottom which is good for holding instead of a rocky bottom. That type of bottom seems to attract lobster pots. Water is flat calm here at 8:45 p.m., with a few mosquitoes.

The next day, was warm and sunny, a good day to haul up the bedding and cushions to air out on deck. After lunch we went ashore to find a lot of large boulders and sandy beach. On the opposite side of the island was a wide crescent sand beach. I found a medium size tree among some boulders, and planted my beach chair there. I spent a few hours just reading and napping, while Marion beachcombed for rocks and shells. Later, we walked together along the beach. About 5:00, it was time to head back to the boat. The tide had come in so far, that the rock we had tied the skiff to, was now under water. Those 10-foot tides are amazing. It's another calm night aboard.

The next morning, on pulling up the anchor, it was coated with sticky mud, so that might explain the lack of lobster pots. Our next stop would be an island we had stopped at before, Hog Island. The wind was light and we motored most of the way. As we neared the Deer Island Bridge, the current picked up against us and soon we were just crawling along. After passing under the bridge we changed direction, and it made the light wind favorable for us, I raised the head sail and shut down the engine. We coasted into our anchorage about 3:45, and dropped the hook in 30 feet of water. Hog Island, here we are again.

An uneventful night at Hog Island, but that's not all bad. We spent the evening reading by candlelight and early to bed. The next morning, was sunny with a little haze that would burn off in a few hours. We got the boat ready to go by clearing off the counter, checking the fuel tank, visual check on the bilge for water and plotting the course for the day. Next stop will be Belfast.

After raising the anchor, Marion steered us out, while I set the main and genoa sails. On the way out of Eggemoggin Reach, we saw a sailboat anchored off two neat islands, one with a pretty sand beach. I made a mental note to stop there next time we pass by. After clearing Cape Rosier, we turned north and got the boat up to four and one half knots, a good rate for us. The main sail was blocking the wind from the genoa sail, making it empty and fill with wind, so we dropped it down till we could turn east. There is an item, called a whisker pole that you attach to the end of the sail and the other end to the mast. This keeps the sail out in position all the time. However, I have yet to make one for the boat. When we reached the north end of Islesboro Island, on our port side, we could turn east and raise the genoa again.

Now with a beam reach, our fastest point of sail, our speed increased to six and one half knots. It's about as fast as we can go and it was fun to steer. At that speed, the boat reacts to a slight movement of the helm immediately. Six and one half knots, converts to about seven plus miles an hour. That may not sound like much, but throw in some four-foot waves, a brisk wind and some water spray flying around, and there is a feeling that you're moving along pretty well. We sailed right up to the anchorage in Belfast and set the anchor in 20-feet of water at 3:15.

We have been here so many times, that we know exactly where we want to set down. We had been sailing for only four hours, but that seemed like enough for the day. When traveling on the water, conditions can change in a hurry and make an easy trip into a real challenge. We'll take the easy ones, knowing that one day we'll be put to the test.

We put down the anchor and backed down on it, with the engine in reverse. When the boat stops going backwards and starts to swing to one side, means the anchor has dug in. I was having trouble pulling up the heavy forty-five pound anchor and fifty-five feet of three eights chain so Marion would have come forward and help me pull. I, of course, had about one hundred fifty feet of rode, what sailors called anchor rode, attached also, but that wasn't a problem for me. I did have a lighter and shorter chain that I thought would work just as well, so I replaced it with the heavy one before dropping anchor this time. The chain helps keep the anchor parallel to the sea bottom and digging in.

We went ashore to enjoy the Celtic celebration. It was great and a few hours later, as we were sitting on the grass with many other people listening to the good music, a huge wind and rain sprang up. It was so strong, that as we all ran for cover it was actually hard to stay upright and run. We all found shelter in a large tent and a little while later, as the wind went down, the program continued.

I was a little concerned about the boat, so we left right after the end of the program. When we anchor in this harbor, we have to be beyond the mooring fields and that means about a mile or more away from the dock. As we motored out, I knew we had anchored across from a commercial dredger boat. When we came near the dredger, there was no sign of our boat. Quickly I scanned the shore thinking it had blown up on the rocks not too far away, but it wasn't there and we didn't see it on the way out either, among the moored boats. Then Marion's sharp eyes picked out a dark object far out to sea. "Is that it," she asked? "Maybe, let's go check it out," I said. Luckily for us, I had enough gas in the skiff, so if it wasn't our boat, we could still return to shore. It took a while to reach it and sure enough, it was *Indian Summer* happily bobbing sideways out to sea. My lighter chain had not proven heavy enough to keep the anchor plowed into the mud during the heavy wind. As it got into deeper water, the whole anchor system just hung down, not reaching the bottom. It felt like losing your house and finding it again, we were so relieved. I replaced the light anchor with the tried and true heavy one and later found a way to use the sail halyard winch to pull in the more secure system.

Whenever we leave the boat unattended I always worry about the anchor dragging, so I try to keep aware of changing wind conditions while ashore. It's the price one pays for not buying a mooring. A good anchoring system is worth a lot in peace of mind.

I have been rejecting the impulse to add a windless, to electrically pull up the anchor, so now I have a new method, instead of brute force. I have Marion motor up to a point, right over the anchor, by then the rope, or rode like sailors call it, is pulled on deck and I have only anchor and chain to pull up. Now, I use a chain grab hook to latch to the chain and on the grab hook leave enough line to reach the halyard winch. Marion, who is in the cockpit, and will now crank the winch, which pulls the chain and anchor up about 20-feet.

Then I lock the chain from falling back into the sea. Once it is locked, I lift the grab hook off the chain and run it back to the bow and hook on the chain again. It takes about three or four sessions of this before the anchor comes clear of the water and I can jerk it into its holder. Sometimes I can come back to the winch and give Marion a rest. It's slow, but it's a lot easier on the muscles.

    We were really looking forward to our daughter, Sara, her husband, John, and their eight-year-old daughter, Mallori, who live in Kansas, to come visit us on the boat. Sara was the only one of our four children that hadn't spent time on the boat although she had helped me a lot when I was building it. We left Belfast, sailed to Warren Island State Park, and tied up on a mooring for overnight. The Island is about half way between Belfast and Camden, where we planned to meet them. They had flown to Boston, and took a bus to Camden, and would arrive about ten o'clock at night on July 21. We left the mooring and had an uneventful sail to Camden, arriving later in the afternoon. We had to call for a mooring and requested one as close to the docks as possible, since it would be a dark ride in the skiff out to the boat. We were directed to a mooring farther out than we had hoped, due to the size of our boat. They arrived around ten o'clock as planned. I shuttled them to the boat in two trips with the skiff, using a flashlight to find our boat in the dark.

    The next day, we sailed with a fair wind to Warren Island again. We all had a good time exploring the island and wading in the shallow water. Mallori enjoyed looking for shells. We had brought a picnic lunch and found a little shelter while exploring the island, so we ate our lunch there. We returned to the boat and visited about what we had been doing. Marion and Mallori did some painting with a little art kit I had found at a thrift store.

When we left in the morning, the wind had turned, and we had a fair wind sailing to Pulpit Rock. It was rainy on and off during the day, but we enjoyed the sail in spite of the rain. John got a chance to handle the boat and seemed to enjoy it. The first time we put the anchor down; we were too close to some rocks and had to move. We didn't go ashore being it was so rainy and wet.

The following day, we sailed back to Camden. The wind was light, and it was more motor sailing than real sailing. Marion wanted to show Mallori and Sara a dollhouse store that Mallori really liked. John and I just spent some time in town and took the shuttle back to the boat.

The next day, we sailed to Rockport which is close to Camden. We spent the day exploring the town and found the library where we spent some time. We asked about a good place to eat, and were directed to a small place we could walk to. We all enjoyed lobster rolls, a first for the landlubbers from Kansas. Then back to the boat before dark. Early the next morning, the fog was so thick I had to use the GPS when I took Sara, John, and Mallori in to the port, where they met a taxi to take them to the bus station in Camden. It had been so much fun having them on the boat, and Mallori said it was the most fun she had ever had. We hated to see them leave.

Later in the day, my old sailing buddy, Roger Anderson, and a friend of his, Jim Miller, arrived from Minneapolis. They had driven out to Maine making stops along the way. They planned to sail with us for just a few days. The first day, we sailed through one of the cuts through an island south of Pulpit Rock. We anchored off one small town, and went ashore to spend the day exploring. While checking out the town, Marion noticed a sign for a thrift store that was open only a couple hours a week on Wednesday. She was happy it was Wednesday, so she could check it out later. I spent my time at the library, and she met me there later. Roger and Jim wandered around town for a while, and I took them back to the boat early so they could rest.

We sailed to the other side of the island, went north, and anchored for the night in a bay. It was a very pleasant evening with a beautiful sunset. It just made one happy to be on the water. The next day, was really foggy in the morning, so we started sailing later, when the fog had lifted somewhat. We motored and sailed around the north end of the island and back to Rockland. We went ashore and explored a bit. Jim and Roger bought us a wonderful supper at one of the many restaurants. The next morning, I took them in after fixing the outboard motor that refused to start. It had been fun and interesting having them on the boat. It had been Roger's third time sailing with me, but sailing was all new to Jim. They insisted on doing the dishes for Marion after each meal, and she thought that was so nice of them. After they left, we sailed directly to Belfast.

July 28, and its hot and sunny. Good day to do laundry, so we got in about 12:00. The laundry house is not far from the dock. We have a mile ride in the skiff first, then an uphill walk for a few blocks pulling the clothes. Before we did this, we got to take showers at the dock, two bucks a person, unlimited water usage. What a deal. While the clothes were being washed, we walked over to the library to check our e-mail and read the newspaper. Sometimes I feel like a homeless person, but there is a strange feeling of freedom too. Later, we would meet up with our friend, Debbie Reynolds, whom we met earlier on our visit to Belfast. There was a concert taking place at the gazebo near the skiff dock, so we packed the clean clothes in the skiff and walked back to the park to listen to the music. So ends the day.

The next day, we got to town early, Marion had spied a garage sale sign, and even though it was a hike up there, she was game to go. I consider garage sales akin to catnip for Marion, just too hard to pass up. Once in a while, I'll find something I don't need to buy, but mostly just go along for company. She found stuff, and we hiked back to town, luckily it was downhill. We caught the city bus and rode it to the pharmacy and grocery store. We got our shopping done in record time and just caught the last bus back to the dock. The friendly driver named Chip gave us good information on the bus routes. It seems that it's almost a secret as to when the bus runs. Even the information people didn't know anything about it and no list of its stops. I guess most everyone has their own transportation here.

The sail back to the marina was uneventful, we stopped to anchor and wait the tide at Ft. Point. We had about nine miles to go upriver and the current can run up to six knots so we really needed to catch the upriver current. In the morning, I woke feeling very sick and didn't feel like we could make the early run up the river. I took some meds and slept for a few more hours. The next current would be at 4:00 p.m. We made use of the waiting time to strip off the sails, as we would be motoring the whole way. We did get the 4:00 turn of the current, and by 7:00 p.m., we were tied up at the marina. That was on a Thursday, and I knew the marina didn't work on weekends, so I was really hoping to get hauled out the next day, Friday. It was rainy, but at high tide, the only time I can get floated over the hydraulic trailer, 1:00 p.m., it had stopped for a bit and they got me out before it began raining hard the rest of the day. We spent Saturday to Monday stripping the lines, sails, cockpit lockers, helm and then putting things away. Marion left for a while to visit a relative of a friend. We drove out on Tuesday for Minnesota.

Reflections

I'm asked many times, was it worth it? Taking all the time and money to build the boat, learn sailing, navigation, collect the charts, find the crew, and so much more, when instead I could have bought a ticket and flew over to Europe and did some of the same things. The ones, who ask the question, probably wouldn't understand my answer. "The voyage, which included everything from 1985 to 2013, is what I wanted. The arriving was not as important as the process of getting there." This of course is not a new idea; others have it too, like mountain climbers or distant runners to name a few. I'm not saying this is what everyone should do, only what I felt I should do, but I only can hope those who sailed with me got something from it also.

As I write this, April 2014, I have no plans to sail this summer due to some other obligations I've taken on. It takes me a while to plan a trip worth the time and money to do so. That will be my goal this year. Maybe by next year, I will have a plan.

Made in the USA
San Bernardino, CA
03 March 2016